American Religious Empiricism

SUNY Series in Religious Studies
Robert C. Neville, Editor

AMERICAN
RELIGIOUS
EMPIRICISM

William Dean

State University of New York Press

Published by
State University of New York Press, Albany

©1986 State University of New York

For information, address State University of New York
Press, State University Plaza, Albany, N.Y., 12246

10 9 8 7 6 5 4 3 2 1

Library of Congress Cataloging-in-Publication Data

Dean, William.
    American religious empiricism.

    (SUNY series in religious studies)
    Includes index.
    1. Empirical theology—Addresses, essays, lectures.
2. Theology, Doctrinal—United States—History—20th
century—Addresses, essays, lectures.   3. Chicago
School of theology— Addresses, essays, lectures.
I. Title. II. Series.
BT83.53.D43 1986   230   85-27769
ISBN 0-88706-280-6
ISBN 0-88706-281-4 (pbk.)

To the theologians of the Chicago School

To make a start,
out of particulars

William Carlos Williams, *Paterson*

Contents

Preface   ix

Acknowledgments   xv

Introduction: The Context of American Religious
Empiricism   1

1. An Empirical Interpretation: An American Theology   19

2. An Historicist Interpretation: The Deconstruction
and Reconstruction of Religious Knowledge   41

3. A Pragmatic Interpretation: The Tragedy of the
Liberals   67

4. An Aesthetic Interpretation: The Elusive "It"   87

5. A Formal Interpretation: The Fate of an American
Theology   101

Notes   119

Index   143

Preface

Sydney Ahlstrom could properly begin his *Theology in America* by saying that American theology was "like a conversation being continued by people as they walk into another room."[1] In the new room, however, the conversation took a new twist. It is on this, on what is novel in the American room, that I focus, rather than on the continuities in the house of Western religious thought. I write out of the conviction that this novelty fits America, that something about American experience once evoked it and still needs it.

This distinctively American approach, American religious empiricism, was implicit in the work of Jonathan Edwards, it was theologically extended by the more empirical of the eighteenth and nineteenth century "Enlightenment Christians," and it was carried on by certain liberal religious thinkers around the turn of the nineteenth century. American religious empiricism was philosophically extended first by William James, then by John Dewey and Alfred North Whitehead, and theologically elaborated by members of the Chicago School of theology, as well as by several twentieth century theologians at Yale and elsewhere in the nation. Today's process theology and a few other theological writings could be treated as participants in the tradition of American religious empiricism. Further, much postmodern thought can be seen as an unknowing revival of America's own almost forgotten empirical tradition. Postmodernism in much of the arts (beginning with William Carlos Williams) echoes the themes of

American religious empiricism, as does postmodernism in literary theory (particularly deconstructionism), in philosophy (particularly Jacques Derrida and Richard Rorty), and in the sciences (particularly John Wheeler).

The following "Introduction" and chapters each use the postmodern standpoint to show American religious empiricism's distinct implication: that history constructs reality, that history is simply a chain of interpretations, and that whatever might lie outside history lies outside religion, empirically considered. The postmodernists and the founders of American religious empiricism agree that history is important, in the broadest sense of the term, religiously. Together, they believe that when a people reinterprets its history it becomes a new people, just as the ancient Hebrews and Christians had believed that when they reinterpreted their former covenant with God they assumed a new covenent with God and became a new people. Equally, the postmodernists and American religious empiricists believe that when history reinterprets a people a new people is created, just as the Hebrews and Christians had believed that when God reinterpreted them, they became new.

In my telling of the story of American religious empiricism, I refer continually to the twentieth century theological expression of American religious empiricism. And here I focus on only one strand of theological expressions: The University of Chicago's "Chicago School" of theology, principally, the theologies of Shailer Mathews and Shirley Jackson Case, and the process theologies most directly connected to it, the empirical process theologies of Henry Nelson Wieman, Bernard Meland, and Bernard Loomer. Process theology is the most important development in contemporary American philosophical theology.[2] It is influenced historically by Christian and Jewish tradition and, among other ideas, by evolutionary theory and relativity theory, particularly as the latter two ideas are interpreted by William James and Alfred North Whitehead; it is based metaphysically on the belief that the "real" is an interrelational process rather than a deep and static substance or structure; it is engendered epistemologically by radical empiricism and by a priori rationalism. I comment repeatedly on process theology and on

Whitehead, who figures centrally in the debate about whether process theology will move toward empiricism, in the direction indicated by American religious empiricism, or whether it will move ever further away from empiricism, in the direction indicated by the rationalism of Charles Hartshorne. I focus on the Chicago School because I think it may be to a distinctively American religious identity what Bruce Kuklick says the Harvard Philosophy Department was to a distinctively American philosophical identity. In *The Rise of American Philosophy*, Kuklick contends that for a period of seventy years the history of American thought could be seen as Harvard's Philosophy Department writ large. He acknowledges that it is an exaggeration to say, as one commentator said, that "the whole of American philosophy" is "but the lengthening shadow of that one great department."[3] It is an even greater exaggeration to say that the whole of American religious thought is but the lengthening shadow of the Chicago School. Nevertheless, one strand of American religious thought has kept returning to the problematic of the Chicago School: history and its religious burden.

Further, just as Kuklick finds in American philosophy a constant direction, toward professionalization, I find in American religious thought a constant direction, toward historicism—a historicism first explicated in the Chicago episode of American religious empiricism. I say this, and yet am aware that religious historicism is hardly known to be the growing trend in twentieth century religious thought, just as professionalization is something about which American philosophers seem not much concerned.

It is true that, instead of focusing on the Chicago School, I could have taken Douglas Clyde Macintosh, H. Richard Niebuhr, and Randolf Crump Miller at Yale as instances of twentieth century American religious empiricism. Or I could have fastened on certain developments at New York's Union Theological Seminary, particularly the work of Daniel Day Williams and James Alfred Martin. Or I could have treated them all together, and included also the work of William H. Bernhardt, Harvey H. Potthoff, and Charles S. Milligan at Iliff School of Theology. I focus, however, on Chicago not only because most of these people depend on Chicago. I focus on Chicago because it is necessary to be selective if the story is to be told in any detail; and if selectivity is required, then Chicago is the best single institution for the job. However, I abbreviate even the Chicago story, for in many respects it continues into the present, in the work of Langdon Gilkey, David Tracy, Don Browning, Franklin Gamwell, Jerald Brauer, and Martin Marty.

I must emphasize that my treatment of even my select few people is never more than a sketch, seeking to note a few of their common points in order to establish that continuity in American thought which allows one to speak of an American religious empiricism. Here my task is not to provide a rounded treatment of these people, not to describe their dissimilarities or even all their similarities, and not to set them carefully into their historical contexts.

To the extent to which this sketch succeeds, to that extent will it evoke a healthy dissatisfaction. While the sketch itself admits to limits, its work within those limits calls for work beyond those limits. The common points it draws are points about method and epistemology; these were the issues over which the identity of American religious empiricism was fought, and in terms of which it was established. Nevertheless, once these points are made, the natural response is to demand how, less abstractly, the affective, the moral, the religious, the aesthetic and, most of all, the historical applications of these points are to be worked out. What is the valuational program implied in American religious empiricism? What are its religious uses? What were and are the historical and active uses of this stance? These are the proper questions and the proper sources of dissatisfaction. Yet their answers can be only intimated here, within this more specific undertaking.

Still, limitation is the mother of consistency. The idea of interpretation grew in importance as I worked on this book, so that, finally, interpretation determines not only the content, but even the form of this book. If the key to American religious empiricism is historicism, then the key to historicism is interpretation. In the literature here discussed, interpretation is to history what substance was to the Aristotelian world. Any writer sympathizing with this literature has the obligation to recognize that fact, for a writer is an interpreter and interpreting has effects, good or bad. Conscious of this fate, I have cast the chapters in the form of explicit interpretations. Each chapter is an interpretation, and the "Introduction" is comprised of three interpretations. Each interpretation can be read independently, and each covers some of the material covered in other interpretations. But rather than add redundancies, each interpretation should add what only a new interpretation can add—in this case, something new from one of the various methodological standpoints of American religious empiricism. The book's own multiple interpretative form replicates synchronically what its content suggests happens diachronically, in the history of a distinctively American chain of religious thought.

Acknowledgments

$\mathbf{M}$y enrollment in a national college of inquiry, which convened in mailboxes, on phone lines and, sometimes (all too rarely), under solid roofs, made this book possible. There I was drawn to radical empiricism, neopragmatism, new historicism, deconstructionism, pluralism, and empirical aesthetics, all as they pertain distinctly to American experience. Bernard Meland and Bernard Loomer have been effective both early and late, twenty or more years ago and again in recent years. In a 1980 conference on process thought and aesthetics, sponsored by the University of British Columbia and the Center for Process Studies and organized by David Griffin, I received from Ekbert Faas, Conrad Hillberry, and Robin Blaser the encouragement this project originally needed. Nancy Frankenberry has helped me to correct weaknesses of concept and expression. Bernard Lee, Giles Gunn, Tony Sherrill, Roland Delattre, Cornel West, Donald Sherburne, and Don Browning have offered over and over the innocent comment which became the knowing analysis.

My work in a conventional college, a college of liberal arts, has made this book possible in another way. In addition to consulting with colleagues in a large and capable religion department, I have conversed daily with faculty and students from all across this college. I would second Richard Bernstein's contention that the liberal arts college is uniquely suited to humanistic studies. For Bernstein is right when he says that humanistic studies, "as their long tradition reveals, require an ambience where talk and dialogue are cultivated, where one feels free to pursue issues and problems that transgress conventional academic boundaries, and where one directly experiences the challenges and encounters that come from colleagues and students with diverse intellectual concerns."* At Gustavus Adolphus College I must thank especially Richard Fuller, Elmer Suderman, and Clair Johnson for bibliographical help, Conrad Hyers for editorial help, Robert Karsten for an odd suggestion which contributed to the form of this book, John Kendall for being a living pragmatist, Janine Genelin for typing, Floyd Martinson for oversight, and Richard Elvee for creating through his conversation in late-afternoon, winter-darkening offices exactly that ambience Bernstein notes.

Three of the chapters which follow are based on three of my articles: Chapter 1 on "An American Theology" in *Process Studies* (Summer 1982); Chapter 2 on "Deconstruction and Process Theology" in *The Journal of Religion* (January 1984); and Chapter 4 on "Whitehead's Other Aesthetic" in *Process Studies* (Spring 1983).

Patricia and Colin and Jennifer genially accepted the absence of mind and body this book required. Gustavus Adolphus College generously provided research monies and time for work on this book. Credit for the "Index" goes to John Poole, who compiled it. The manuscript was developed and virtually completed while I was Research Fellow at the Institute for the Advanced Study of Religion at The University of Chicago in 1984-85.

---

*Richard J. Bernstein, *Beyond Objectivism and Relativism: Science, Hermeneutics, and Praxis* (Philadelphia: University of Pennsylvania Press, 1983), p.xvii.

Introduction: The Context of American Religious Empiricism

. . . faith in a fact can help create the fact . . .[1]

Although the history of American religious empiricism exists as a chain of concrete historical events, it can be defined only abstractly. It is found where certain ideas are voiced. Like other religious orientations, it seeks a reason for living by referring to some world character or purpose, described by the word "God." And like other religious orientations it recurs to distinctive ideas: that we believe what we experience (empiricism); that we experience more than we can scientifically describe, and, consequently, that we look to the broadest range of phenomena (natural and social history); that history is alive, and is built through the present generation's perception of its past and its act of revision (interpretation); and that we interpret by introducing new ideas, looking to what might be with a sense of trust (faith).

These ideas characterize what Daniel Day Williams calls "a vein of religious thought and attitude which runs underneath the surface of much American Christianity."[2] Williams goes on to say, "Perhaps the most important root of theological empiricism was the belief, derived from the Christian faith and present in the American consciousness from the Puritans and Edwards to the present, that a sufficiently faithful and realistic attention to the direction of historical event will disclose the hand and judgment of God."[3]

1

I will introduce American religious empiricism not by elaborating further its content, but by identifying three of its contexts. I will show its antecedents in ancient Hebrew thought, its development in American liberal religious thought, and its contemporary setting in American post-modern thought. At the outset I should stress that this discussion makes no effort to serve as an objective historical explanation. Rather, it merely locates religious empiricism in several contexts, and does that with an openly interpretive bias.

The Hebrew Origins of American Religious Empiricism

The story of Job manifests the paradigm of interpretation more clearly than perhaps any other passage in the Hebrew Bible. If interpretation is the act of construing something new out of what is given by the past, then oddly, in *Job* it is the natural and social history surrounding Job which accomplish the first interpretation. Natural disasters and social calamities make something new out of the man Job. They interpret Job as a man beset with unwarranted suffering. Job's counselors then unsuccessfully interpret this interpretation of Job. But the story focuses on Job's own interpretation of history's interpretation of him. Job finds in history an expression of the mystery of God, to which Job must respond in an act of trust.

The Hebrew Bible works largely with these two sides of interpretation: natural and social history interpret Israel, and Israel interprets that history as an expression of God. The stories of the exodus, the settlement, the kingship, and the accounts of the prophets all work with these two sides of interpretation, but focus on social history. The stories of the wisdom writers work similarly with interpretation, but focus on natural history. Israel learns as much by seeing how history interprets it, as by seeing how it should interpret history. The recurring idea of the Hebrew Bible is that the key to interpretation is Israel's God. The Hebrew Bible argues both that history's interpretation of Israel is best understood when seen as affected by God, and that Israel's acts in history are best accomplished when they seek to respond to the God working through that same history.

Gerhard Von Rad argues that God's interpretation of Israel should be seen as as a covenant act. God works through natural history and social history to reach a nation bound to God in a covenant relation. The separate events of natural and social history are connected as temporal moments in a continuous, evolving covenant relatedness. In this sequence God's power over history is derived from God's power over nature; this is especially clear when God's power over nature is manifest in God's acts of creation (Von Rad cites Jeremiah 27:4ff and Isaiah 45:12ff).[4]

Israel, however, should not merely observe God extending the covenant promise and judgment through natural and social history. Israel should also respond to God through new interpretations of that natural and social history. In fact, Von Rad contends that "the only possible subject of a theology of the Old Testament" is faith: specifically, the "grounding of Israel's faith upon a few divine acts of salvation and the effort to gain an ever new understanding of them."[5] Von Rad rejects as largely irrelevant the "scientific" theologies of the Hebrew Bible, which attempt to unify the Hebrew Bible under the heading of doctrines such as the doctrine of God and the doctrine of human nature. He rejects as incomplete the "modern historical scholarship," which is content to provide new factual information about the history of Israel, but which fails adequately to portray Israel's evolving understanding of its history. Von Rad's "tradition history" approach, initiated in 1938,[6] sees the Hebrew Bible as a sequence of new interpretations by Israel of the events in its past. These interpretations are found in creeds, sacral laws, cultic texts, and in ritual. They are set down in units as small and as early as the confessional summary of Deuteronomy 26:5-9, beginning "A wandering Aramean was my father," and as large and as late as the grand compilations which are the Hexateuch, the Deuteronomistic history, and the Chronicler's history. These interpretations are empirical in that they attempt to respond to the events of history and nature; they are valuational in that they point to the divine presence in the events of nature and history.[7]

For many Hebrews, then, what is real in the deepest sense is nothing but a sequence of evolving interpretations. This sequence of interpretations, whether by natural and social history or by the Hebrew spokesperson, is deadly serious. There is nothing beyond it which gives salvation and security. Reality is not composed of something static, whether divine or human, which could be doctrinally set forth; reality is not composed of positivistic facts, which a modern historical scholar might isolate. Instead, the Hebrew community lives with a changing God, who interprets the Hebrews differently in different times. And the Hebrew community itself is a changing community, which interprets its nature, its history, and its God differently in different times. The ancient Hebrew community and its God lived in a relation of mutual interpretation. They lived in history, nothing more. There was no escape.

It follows that the Hebrew Bible and even the New Testament are authoritative not because of their static "truths," but because of their process. They use a canonizing process to show the process of a developing people relating to a developing God. Robert B. Laurin, citing Samuel Sandmel, distinguishes canonizing from canonization. The typical practice for the ancient Hebrews was "canonizing," meaning the process whereby the tradition was freshly applied to historical situations as they arose. The Hebrews did not isolate and authorize a particular scriptural form or theological ideal; rather, they included diverse forms and ideals among their traditions and used them as they were appropriate, for "each generation heard God's will for themselves."[8] They included, for example, both the Deuteronomist's and the Chronicler's histories, inconsistent as they might be, because interpretations of those writings might contribute to the movement with Yahweh to *shalom*. The New Testament and the early church continued the canonizing process, as the New Testament writer and the early church used the Hebrew Bible, not for what it meant for the Hebrew writers in their day, but for what it meant for the early Christian community in its day. The subsequent "canonization," the closure of the canonizing process and the freezing of interpretations, represented a change in this original attitude. It was the abandonment, says Laurin, of the "dynamic dialogue between tradition and community" inspired by a God who "was dynamic and developing his will."[9]

Two groups of biblical scholars have extended both Von

Rad's tradition history and the concept of the canonization process. First, there are those who seek rather conventionally to amplify Von Rad's method. Some of them have contributed to the anthology, Tradition and Theology in the Old Testament, published in 1977 and edited by Douglas Knight. This collection includes Laurin's essay on canonization, and takes as precedents not only Von Rad's method but Martin Noth's practice in his A History of the Pentateuchal Traditions. The editor notes that "the tradition process creates new meaning,"[10] and advocates the theory of interpretation which dominates the anthology. Second, there is the recent sociological approach, which shows how social needs of biblical communities evoked a particular historical interpretation, which in turn worked as a creative force in the biblical religions and scriptures. This sociological approach is well illustrated in another anthology, The Bible and Liberation: Political and Social Hermenuetics, edited by Norman Gottwald and published in 1976. The authors not only demonstrate the social base of religious interpretation, but contend that the interpretation was shaped by the motif of liberation from oppression. The authors lift this motif out of the biblical world and use it to construct a third world liberation theology for today. Gottwald elaborates that argument in his The Tribes of Israel: A Sociology of the Religion of Liberated Israel, 1250–1050 (1979). A straight sociological analysis, without the liberation motif, is exercised most notably by John G. Gager in his Kingdom and Community: An Anthropological Approach to Civilization (1975) and Wayne Meeks in his The First Urban Christians: The Social World of the Apostle Paul (1983). With or without the liberation motif, however, the sociological approach presumes that biblical religions and their sacred writings were interpretations of social circumstances.

American Religious Empiricism as Liberal

Religious empiricism in America falls within the broad range of Christian liberalism, which treats the experience of the religious person as the first and basic authority. The liberal treats the Bible, creeds, dogmas, liturgies, or policies as authoritative only when they are received as authoritative in human experience. The liberal looks to an evolving and interpreted record of human experience, set in history and reinterpreted for present history. The Bible and the ecclesiastical writings are seen, then, in and for history. When the American religious empiricists treat historical experience as authoritative, they agree with the German liberals from the early nineteenth century onwards.

However, American religious empiricism differs from German liberalism in having a more thorough historicism. For Friedrich Schleiermacher religious self-consciousness is a historical phenomenon, and it is the functional authority which supercedes all authoritative literatures. However, Schleiermacher never claimed that God is itself a historical reality, let alone a changing and interpreting activity. Schleiermacher's Absolute is an eternal, immutable reality existing beyond history, impervious to the effects of history. In short, Schleiermacher's liberalism is halfway to a thorough historicism; for Schleiermacher the religious subject is historical but the historical object, God, stands beyond history. American religious empiricism, by comparison, usually insists that both the religious subject and the religious object are historical. To recognize this difference I will call Schleiermacher's liberalism "pietistic liberalism" and American religious empiricism "empirical liberalism."[11]

The distinctness of each liberalism can be very briefly sketched. The God of the pietistic liberals could be nonhistorical because the pietists accepted a realm of spirit, separate from the events of natural and social history. The God of the pietists could exist in this nonhistorical realm and still be accessible to natural and social history by means of the spiritual experience of the religious subject. By contrast, the God of the empirical liberals could not be nonhistorical because (in principle, if not always in terminology) they had replaced this nature-spirit dualism with a nature-spirit unity in which whatever might be called spirit lies within, not beyond, history. For the empirical liberals God has no spiritual and nonhistorical dwelling place, and must dwell in history. The origin of the difference between the two types of liberals can be explained by tracing the pietistic liberals to Kant in particular and by tracing the empirical liberals to the British

Enlightenment of the late seventeenth and the early eighteenth centuries.

The term "pietistic" is derived from the German sectarian pietism which led Kant to protect piety by placing it within a realm of subjective knowing independent of the world as it is in itself.[12] When Kant admitted that the world as it is in itself could not be known, he acknowledged that God in the external worlds of natural and social history could not be known. God is manifest, however, in the spiritual and practical reason of the human subject. In this, Kant set the agenda for many of the nineteenth century theologians—which is not to claim that these theologians were always Kantian or neo-Kantian. These theologians, greatly different in other ways, did agree among themselves and with Kant in dividing their vision between a historical self and a nonhistorical God. Friedrich Schleiermacher's emphasis on feeling, Hegel's emphasis on reason, Albrecht Ritschl's emphasis on the moral will, and Ernst Troeltsch's emphasis on the historical community are all forms of pietistic liberalism, and they all point to a self in history related to a God beyond history.

The pietistic liberalism of these thinkers was accepted by many nineteenth and twentieth century American preachers and theologians. The American Transcendentalist movement generally, and Ralph Waldo Emerson in particular, despite their new attention to the immediacies of human experience, emphasized a rational intuition, capable of seeing through the subject's natural and social history an absolute beyond history. Horace Bushnell transmitted pietistic liberalism up to its full flowering among the American clergy of the late nineteenth and early twentieth century, when there appeared such major proponents as William Newton Clarke, William Adams Brown, the Boston Personalists, and Walter Rauschenbush. Josiah Royce, despite his concern with experience and its pragmatic meaning, gave philosophical prominence to pietistic liberalism by generating an idealistic philosophy of religion. The most important twentieth century American pietistic liberal was Paul Tillich, whose use of Friedrich Schelling and existentialism, and whose development of the concept of faith and symbol all suggest an approach to a nonhistorical God through the experience of an historical subject.

Tillich was a liberal, building his theology on an analysis of the faith experience,[13] and at the same time he was a liberal who could contend that "it belongs to the nature of the ultimate to be beyond time and space."[14]

The empirical liberals generally rejected the nature-spirit duality typical of pietistic liberalism, accepted a nature-spirit unity, and consequently became more thoroughly historicist, placing God as well as the religious self within the dynamics of history. Both their reason for doing this and their difference from the pietistic liberals is best appreciated by an examination of their philosophical and theological lineage.

The empirical liberals were children of the British empirical Enlightenment. They, with other Enlightenment thinkers, accepted what Henry May, in his *The Enlightenment in America*, calls the two major propositions on which the Enlightenment was based: "first, that the present age is more enlightened than the past; and second, that we understand nature and man best through the use of our natural faculties."[15] But as empiricists the empirical liberals argued through the use of careful observation rather than through the use of wit—the primary tool of the French and skeptical Enlightenment thinkers such as Voltaire. Also, they were more preoccupied with epistemology than with questions of social organization—the primary topic for such revolutionary Enlightenment thinkers as Rousseau and Paine. John Locke was the grandfather of the empirical liberals, and David Hume was the father against whom they staged an in-house and contained rebellion.

The empirical Enlightenment, and the British empirical Enlightenment in particular, gave to the empirical liberals an epistemological monism: the belief that "natural faculties" were directed to the world which science had opened in the seventeenth century, and the belief that there was no world beyond that world. First, the empirical Enlightenment had rejected the spirit world of the church; later it rejected the spirit world of the Kantians, the neo-Kantians, and the idealists. It was this nondualistic and unified nature-spirit world which the empirical liberals inherited and which allowed them to avoid the dualisms of the pietistic liberals.

Although the empirical liberals were led to their one world by the British empiricists, these liberals moved beyond Locke's and Hume's characterization of the world as accessible only by the five senses, and as value-free. They claimed that we perceive also affectionally, through moral, religious and aesthetic experience; and they created thereby a broader empiricism which James would call a "radical empiricism." The important point here, however, is that they continued to work with the general epistemology and cosmology of the British empiricists, and refused to become dualists once they became convinced that moral and religious and aesthetic experience could be valid experience of the external world. For the empirical liberals, then, God had to work within the world of natural and social history or not work at all. This is recognized with lesser or greater explicitness by a succession of thinkers beginning with Jonathan Edwards, who expanded Locke's empiricism to include a "sense" of beauty,[16] and William James, who revolted from Herbert Spencer's positivistic and materialistic empiricism, not by leaving empiricism, but by adding to Spencer's five senses various forms of affectional perception.[17]

American religious empiricism grew in a thin but continuous and distinctive strand. The late eighteenth and early nineteenth century Unitarians developed a Newtonian natural theology. While some Unitarians accepted a Transcendentalist idealism, others embraced even more tightly an empirical natural theology informed largely by Locke. Darwinism then overshadowed both the Unitarian version of supernatural revelation and, more particularly, the Unitarian natural theology, replacing a God-revealing nature with a "nature red in tooth and claw." However, men such as Newman Smyth and Charles A. Briggs soon attempted to show the congruity between Christianity and the newest advances in the sciences. This emphasis carried into the Divinity School of the University of Chicago, beginning in the early twentieth century. Here the Chicago School of theology was developed; it included the work of Ernest Dewitt Burton, George Burman Foster, Shailer Mathews, Gerald Birney Smith, Edward Scribner Ames, and Shirley Jackson Case.[18] Douglas Clyde Macintosh studied at Chicago and devoted his career at

Yale to expounding an empirical theology, affecting such theologians as H. Richard Niebuhr and Randolph Crump Miller. William Henry Bernhardt began as a student at Chicago and had much the same sort of major effect at Iliff School of Theology, heavily influencing Harvey Potthoff and Charles Milligan. Daniel Day Williams moved from Chicago to New York's Union Theological Seminary, defending empirical liberalism in a largely neo-orthodox environment, and working with James Alfred Martin, another empirical liberal. During this midcentury period Henry Nelson Wieman, Bernard Meland, and Bernard Loomer became at Chicago those process theologians who worked most explicitly within the empirical tradition of the Chicago School. Meland, in his "Introduction" to a volume entitled *The Future of Empirical Theology* and containing papers read at Chicago in 1966, distinguished the Chicago School and the empirical theologies from what I am calling pietistic liberalism. He said that the former retained an interest in "literal processes of divinity being observed,"[19] while the latter contained "something of the earlier Platonistic notion of reality casting its shadow upon concrete experience."[20]

Meland's comment suggests the most dangerous but perhaps the simplest and most helpful distinction between the pietistic and the empirical liberals, the distinction between idealism and empiricism. The pietistic liberals were idealists because, at bottom, they regarded spirit (mentality, *geist*) as the key to either or both epistemology and metaphysics, answering how we know and what we know, whereas the empirical liberals were empiricists because they regarded sense experience, broadly interpreted, as the key.

The distinction between idealism and empiricism can indicate lines of pietistic and empirical thinkers, and thus better reveal the general drift of these thinkers. For example, although Emerson does attend to the affective experience of nature and to the peculiar nuance of American experience, his thought is indelibly idealistic. Emerson could say that "the intellect searches out the absolute order of things as they stand in the mind of God, and without the colors of affection."[21] Recognizing that "Children, it is true, believe in the external world,"[22] Emerson goes on to claim that now we know "the eternal distinction between the soul and the world."[23] Again, Emerson argues that "empirical science is apt to cloud the sight, and by the very knowledge of functions and processes to bereave the student of the manly contemplation of the whole."[24] Or, Josiah Royce also might at first appear to be an empirical liberal, for he does reject a merely contemplative idealism. But, says John E. Smith, "The perplexing fact is that Royce emphasized the will and rejected the so-called pure intellect without seeming to come any closer to the pragmatic philosophy of his contemporaries [Peirce, James, and Dewey]."[25] Royce finally could say, "If the more my mind grows in mental clearness, the nearer it gets to the nature of reality, then surely the reality my mind thus resembles must be in itself mental."[26] Royce, says Bruce Kuklick, "was a Kantian intrigued by Berkeley."[27]

While the distinction between idealism and empiricism can function to place unambiguously certain people within idealism, it can place, equally, certain other people within empiricism, and, thus, identify them as empirical liberals. For example, James might appear at first to be an idealist, because for James mind is not entirely passive and does not create in part the world.[28] It is true that idealism did argue for the priority of mind. However, this similarity with idealism is far overshadowed by James's dependence on John Locke, who contended above all else that ordinary knowledge begins in sense experience. When James argued for the creativity of mind, he argued for the creativity of a nature-spirit self within a nature-spirit world. When, however, the idealists claimed the creativity of mind, they argued for the creativity of spirit within a world of spirit. While James treated mental creativity as a random or volitional and experimental variation within a world of natural selectivity, the idealists looked at mental creativity as a rational construct within a world of rational constructs. For James mental creativity placed humans closer to biological nature, while for the idealists creativity placed humans farther above biological nature. Finally, the idealist-empiricist distinction shows why it is impossible to place a thinker such as William Ernest Hocking, one who borrows from both Royce and James, either clearly outside of or clearly within empirical liberalism.

American religious empiricism, then, is part of a liberal

tradition which looks to human experience and its interpretations as authoritative, and looks at its God as living within
history. In these ways that movement is part of a distinctively
American empirical Enlightenment. Joseph Haroutunian near the
end of his career pointed out the empirical and pragmatic strand
in American religious thought and argued for the fuller amplification of the historical context I have only sampled:

> In fact, it is doubtful that there is prospect for American
> theology at all without a new knowledge of the history of
> theology in this country. America may not have produced an
> Augustine or a Schleiermacher, but its hope of producing theol-
> ogians who shall do more than live off the European mind has
> little chance of being realized unless the history of theology in
> America is studied, not as a tributory of European theology, but,
> for all its derivative character, as an expression of American
> experience.[29]

American Religious Empiricism as Post-Modern

The rise of post-modernism in American arts and letters
during the past fifty years provides a new impetus for a restoration of religious empiricism. Just as in the early twentieth century
James's, Dewey's, and Whitehead's new and radical empiricism
spurred the Chicago School and related forms of theological
empiricism, so today certain post-modern modes of thought in
the arts and in art criticism and in philosophy show the potential
for spurring a resurgence of that same general empiricism.

Any brief characterization of post-modernism in the arts and
philosophy works from a particular standpoint and cannot claim
comprehensive validity. Nevertheless, briefly characterized, post-
modernism can be seen as a new position on the nature of the
interpretive process, distinguished from the modernist and what
might be called the pre-modernist views on the interpretive
process.

Modernism sought, above all, to reject what it saw as the
pre-modern claim that the interpretation of reality is given—by

an authority to a society. When in the seventeenth century Francis Bacon, Kepler, Galileo, and Hobbes set forth their nascent empiricisms, they rejected many of the authoritative interpretations of churches and governments. They and their logical successor, Isaac Newton, held that, while interpretations given by authorities may hold in the religious realm, they cannot hold in the world of nature or politics. In his own way and before them all, Martin Luther had held that even in the religious realm the faith of the individual must take precedence over the policy of the church. These and other English, Italian, French, and German voices rose in an odd chorus, rejecting the notion that the proper interpretation of the world was fixed and given, that it was simply to be received by the people from the hands of institutional authorities, whether those authorities spoke for Greek philosophy, for Palestinian scriptures, for the Roman ecclesiastical authority, or for the monarchy.

Stated positively, modernism intended to replace the givenness of interpretation with various notions of the autonomy of interpretation. For the empiricists, from Bacon, to Locke and Hume, and to Darwin and Ernest Rutherford, interpretations were to be based on the logically connected data of the five senses. For the rationalists, from Descartes, Spinoza, Kant, Hegel, to Albert Einstein, interpretations were to be based on coherent and often speculative thought. For the romanticists, from Rousseau, to the nineteenth century British romantic poets, to the twentieth century existentialists, interpretations were to be based on a special quality of consciousness, usually emotional or volitional in character. For the modernist the autonomy of an interpretation meant that it was based on one's own perception, thought, or emotion. For the modernist, fighting for the autonomy of interpretation and against the pre-modern notion of the givenness of interpretation, the preferred objects of attack were the church and the state.

But interpreted from a post-modern standpoint, modernism seemed unable to live consistently with its proclaimed autonomy. Empiricist modernism tended to drift into positivism, living not on the autonomous freedom of the perceiving knower, but on what were thought to be the physical regularities of nature and the laws of mathematics. Positivists from Auguste Comte to A. J. Ayer became the dominant voices of empiricism. They tended to replace the pre-modern givenness of interpretation derived from the church or the state with a new givenness of interpretation, derived from the authority of science. Rationalistic modernism tended to drift into the veneration of logic, living not on the autonomous freedom of the speculative thinker, but on what were thought to be the logical regularities underlying nature and history. Rationalism tended to elevate the objective logic of the spirit as it operated in history (Hegel), the objective logic of dialectical materialism (Marx), the objective logic of the trans-cendental ego (Husserl), the objective logic of logical atomism (Wittgenstein, Russell), or the objective logic of linguistic struc-ture (Saussure, Chomsky), to name a few of the rationalist expressions. Rationalist modernism replaced the pre-modernist givenness of interpretation with a modernist givenness of inter-pretation, derived from an objectified logic of the world. Much romanticism and existentialism became a shortcut to authoritar-ianism. Romantic modernism sometimes supported a fascist veneration of the political leader. Existentialist modernism some-times supported intellectually humiliating ecclesiastical dogmas. Ironically then, modernism tended to move from its own ideal of autonomous interpretation to a revival of the ideal of the given-ness of interpretation.

Post-modernism is an effort, once again, to throw off the givenness of interpretation. It asserts that interpretation arises in a historical process—namely in the struggle between the object which interprets us and we who interpret the object.

The move into post-modernism is perhaps most vividly seen in literary criticism. Post-modern literary critics reject New Criti-cism and symbolism, both of which can be seen initially as efforts to read autonomously. New Criticism sought to free the reader from a dependence on the historical context or the personality of the author, and to point the reader to a free-standing literary text. Symbolism sought to encourage the reader to see through the literary text to the eternal logos or to the objective meaning it symbolically expresses. However, the post-modern literary critics see in such modernism not autonomy, but a subservience to the

text, to its formal structure, or its logocentric meaning. In an
initial reaction the Yale Critics—including Geoffrey Hartman, J.
Hillis Miller, and Paul de Man—in various and individual ways
argued that literature itself is largely the writer's interpretation of
preceding literature and that the reading of literature is an act of
reader interpretation.[30] At places they suggested the sheer autonomy of the reader; but elsewhere they agreed with their mentor,
Jacques Derrida, and treated reading as an interaction between
the past literary text and the freedom of the present reader. That
post-modern literary ideal of mutual interpretation between past
text and present reader is more apparent in several younger
critics, such as Frank Lentricchia[31] and Charles Altieri.[32]

Ekbert Faas in *Towards a New American Poetics* has argued
through essays and interviews that the post-modern literary
sensibility of the literary critics is based on the pioneering work
of American poets and novelists who gave expression to the
subtle depths of their experiences, which were themselves reinterpretations of the world. Although Faas cites oriental and
European roots, his essay on Charles Olson and his interviews
with Robert Duncan, Gary Snyder, Robert Creeley, Allen Gins-
burg, and Robert Bly demonstrate the strength of the American
artistic leadership.[33] While Faas does not make much of William
Carlos Williams, I believe that all these artists are indebted to
that pioneer, American, post-modern poet.

On the boundary line between literary and philosophical
post-modernism stands Jacques Derrida, who not only called for
the deconstruction of Western logocentric constructions on
literature, but who claimed that meanings are constructed by
interpretations, and that interpretations interpret nothing but
earlier interpretations. If it could be said that Derrida has a
cosmology, his cosmology makes reality a temporal chain of
signifiers, each link interpreting some earlier link, which itself
interprets a still earlier link.[34] Derrida gave real power to the
signifier of the past, claiming not that it was merely passive to the
reader's interpretation, but that it also interpreted the present
reader.

Richard Rorty shows the historical development of philosophical post-modernism in two books, *Philosophy and the Mirror of*

Nature and *Consequences of Pragmatism*.[35] Like Derrida he attacks logocentrism, tracing it back to Descartes and focusing on its belief that the mind mirrors some eternal structure in nature. Positively, Rorty suggests that the fundamental ingredient of the world is interpretations, hermeneutical account upon hermeneutical account, all the way down.

Rorty is only the most recent in a line of post-modern philosophers. Cornel West has argued that the post-modernists in Anglo-American philosophy have surpassed what we are calling pre-modernism and modernism in at least three moves: "the move toward anti-realism or conventionalism in ontology; the move toward the demythologization of the Myth of the Given or anti-foundationalism in epistemology; and the move toward the detranscendentalization of the subject or the dismissal of the mind as a sphere of inquiry."[36] He elaborates these themes by reference to W. V. Quine, Nelson Goodman, Thomas Kuhn, Wilfred Sellers, and Richard Rorty. Elsewhere, Nelson Goodman has argued that the correspondence theory of truth, with its naive realism, is in fact simply one version of the world. Once we recognize that we inhabit many worlds in which different truths hold, then we replace the correspondence theory of truth with the coherence theory, and test notions not only for their coherence but for their applicability to socially entrenched practices.[37] Goodman endorses even John Wheeler's notion of a "participatory universe."[38] Goodman's *Ways of Worldmaking* elaborates this post-modern, pragmatic understanding of truth.[39] Adopting a similar stance are Hilary Putnam in his *Reason, Truth and History* and Richard Bernstein in his *Beyond Objectivism and Relativism*. In introducing a set of articles on and by Goodman, Putnam and Rorty, Daniel Bell characterizes our time as one where the "quest for certainty" has been replaced by a "turn to interpretation."[40] The contemporary hermeneutical era, Bell says, has moved away from both positivism and a search for "laws" or "regularities," and toward the practices of the humanities as they are newly exercised by the social scientist.

Here Bell, in the last analysis, is echoing John Dewey. Richard Rorty notes that in 1930 Dewey wrote,

> Intellectual prophecy is dangerous; but if I read the signs of the times aright, the next synthetic movement in philosophy will

emerge when the significance of the social sciences and arts has become the object of reflective attention in the same way that mathematical and physical sciences have been made the objects of thought in the past, and when their full import is grasped.[41]

In another context Rorty expands the point by saying, "James and Dewey were . . . waiting at the end of the road" down which most analytic and Continental philosophers over the past few decades have been traveling.[42] Rorty refers to such philosophers as Habermas, Foucault, and Deleuze. The irony is that such a major precedent for these European thinkers lies in the work of Americans, even Americans about whom these Europeans are generally ignorant and Americans who can be called American religious empiricists. Add to this the irony that James and Dewey were waiting at the end also of another road, the road down which not only post-modern poets, but other artists were traveling, artists such as Merce Cunningham, Jackson Pollack, Alain Robbes-Grillet, and John Cage, as they suggested a creativity of expression, imitating nothing, but building through reinterpreting the past.

James and Dewey realized and definitively expressed the universal significance of historical interpretation, and described it in a way which echoes the ancient Hebrews as well as anticipates the ensuing rise of post-modern thought. They began by reflections on nature, and then extended them to apply to human mental life. The center of their thinking is their response to Darwin and to the evolutionary thought of their day. Finally, James's pragmatism is a commentary on how a variation is assessed by reference to how it fits into and alters the process of natural selection. Dewey's pragmatism is a commentary on how the present individual's action harmonizes with and yet adds complexity to environments. All natural and human development adds to the environment the individual's interpretation; the resulting new environment in turn becomes part of the objective environment, interpreting later individuals and being reinterpreted by them. There are no standards, norms, or truths beyond this historical interaction between one's history and oneself. In these commentaries James and Dewey move beyond modernism and help to usher in a post-modern agenda.

Chapter 1

An Empirical Interpretation: An American Theology

The contours of American religious empiricism are most vividly seen in the light cast by the British empirical Enlightenment, particularly by the shining precedent of John Locke. This much becomes clear: the distinctively American religious empiricism was a child of British empiricism, limiting knowledge to what can be sensuously experienced. But it was a rebellious child, rejecting some of the boundaries set by its English parent. America's empiricism refused to restrict sensuous experience to the experience of the five senses. American empiricism was radical, more thorough, more tolerant than Britian's, enlarging what is meant by sense experience. To put it differently, for American religious empiricism the scientific model of empiricism was superceded by a more inclusive historical model of empiricism, which included the natural and social and personal dimensions of history.

The irony of American religious empiricism, the factor which always has hobbled it, is that it never followed through. It never developed a definite empiricism for what might be called historical sensations. Consequently, American religious empiricism never grew as it might have grown if it had developed a disciplined sense of history.

In the effort to illustrate these two points, I will narrow the range of figures discussed earlier, and concentrate on only three moments in the chronology of American religious empiricism: the eighteenth century episode which was the work of Jonathan Edwards; the philosophical stabilization of American religious empiricism which came in the work of William James, John Dewey, and Alfred North Whitehead; and the theological stabilization of American religious empiricism which came in the empirical process theologies of Henry Nelson Wieman, Bernard Meland, and Bernard Loomer. By no means am I claiming that these seven philosopher/theologians are exclusively important; their number is limited only to make the story intelligible.

An American Empiricism

Described negatively, the distinctiveness of American radical empiricism lies in its rejection of the closure of both German idealism and eighteenth century British empiricism, including the positivism which grew from that empiricism.[1] Jonathan Edwards followed John Locke in rejecting innate ideas; but Edwards departed from Locke by rejecting Locke's own working notion that knowledge of the external world is derived exclusively by means of the five senses. William James, much later occupying the same Massachusetts soil, stared east and recalled German idealism, British empiricism, and the uneasy French, Cartesian corpus from which, like two arms (one spiritual, one sensuous), they grew. He, in turn, grew uneasy. James, Whitehead, Dewey, and the empirical process theologians all finally rejected not only the Cartesian method, but the one-sidedness of both the German and the British traditions.

It is as though, in typical American fashion, they all looked west, and all saw the prospect for a new beginning with a new openness. It is as though their geography led to their epistemology, and they said, "Cleave to raw experience." It is as though they sought to return to the sources of knowledge, prior to the division into mind and body, self and world. Like Hebrews in the wilderness, they chose that unformed, uninterpreted, physical cacophony of emotional, valuational, largely nonconscious and in every sense ambiguous, objective experience, felt initially and blindly by the body.

Genesis figured largely in their speculations; if the act of knowing is to be understood, they suggested, look more openly to the murky origins of the act. Descartes's criterion of "clear and distinct ideas" is exactly backwards; it selects the late, clean, anemic abstraction, in which what is rich, complicating, unclear, indistinct, and valuable has been already eliminated, leaving only a vapid set of sense data or a vapid set of rational ideas. In reaction to this Cartesian type of intellectualism, radical empiricism was formed. It was an elementary approach to knowledge; its only epistemology was a radical openness to all that enters experience.

Of course, such elementariness made the radical empiricists appear naive. Edwards was open to the idea that the conversion experience could be spotted—albeit fallibly—in the "extraordinary things" in the behavior of converts;[2] James was open to empirical evidence for parapsychological phenomena; Whitehead was open to the idea that the initial, physical response of all creatures was aesthetic. But, for them, being naive was not the problem it had been for the Europeans such as Descartes, who had vowed at the beginning of his *Meditations*, henceforth, to do all he could to avoid wrong opinions. Their aim was not to avoid error, but to find the truth, no matter how vulnerable that quest might make them to the outlandish conclusion. James said of his sympathizers, you will be "ready to be duped many times in your investigation rather than postponing indefinitely the chance of guessing true."[3] Certainly this quest invited chaos, but the radical empiricists had the optimism (James called it the "lightness of heart") to believe that potential chaos could and should be sustained, particularly if the cost of avoiding potential chaos was to limit, in advance, the range of experience.

The radical empiricists, then, rejected both idealism and positivistic empiricism, and did so as a protest against closure of evidence. They sought openness and made it a criterion more important than clarity, even if it flirted with disorder.

Radical empiricism was not, however, merely a third school, standing beside idealism and positivistic empiricism. Rather, it was a revision and expansion of empiricism. The distinctiveness of radical empiricism can be understood through a review of the empirical epistemologies of a select list of thinkers: Edwards, James, Whitehead, and Dewey.

Jonathan Edwards repeatedly refers to, heavily depends upon and, finally, augments John Locke's An Essay Concerning Human Understanding. In simplest terms, Edwards added to the five senses of Locke what Morton White calls a sixth sense, the sense of the heart.[4] Edwards, while rejecting Locke's actual restriction of empiricism to the five senses, accepted Locke's methodological concession that "there may be justly counted" more than the five senses in this "vast and stupendous universe."[5]

Edwards's sense of the heart is a sense, not an opinion, a notion, or a speculation. There is a difference, Edwards said, "between having an opinion, that God is holy and gracious, and having a sense of the loveliness and beauty of that holiness and grace. There is a difference between having a rational judgment that honey is sweet, and having a sense of its sweetness."[6] Certainly, the sense of the heart is an unusual sensation on three counts: first, in the self the sensation is appreciated through the will and, sometimes, the affections, rather than through Locke's dispassionate "perception," which is called "understanding";[7] second, what is sensed is sensed not for any new truth it might provide, but for its value, goodness, amiability, beauty, or their opposites;[8] third, this value does not originate within what is sensed, but in the spirit of God which emanates through what is sensed.[9] Nevertheless, in any particular instance the sense of the heart is a sensation because it is a communication to the self arising from a physical object external to the self. "As for instance," Edwards said, "some men are said to have a sense of the dreadfulness of God's displeasure. This apprehension of God's displeasure is called having a sense and is to be looked upon as a part of sensible knowledge, because of the evil or pain in the object of God's displeasure, that is connected with God's displeasure."[10]

For Edwards, then, the process of salvation depends in part on a process of restoring sensibility. John Locke had claimed that if words are removed from the sensations which gave them meaning, they become meaningless signs; and he had argued that for this meaninglessness the only cure was a renewed acquaintance with empirical sensation.[11] Now Edwards, apparently following the form of Locke's empirical therapy, described sin as the failure of human sensibility, as "the alienation of the inclinations and natural disposition of the soul from those things as they are."[12] Things as they exist are comprehended only through a renewal of "sensible knowledge," and sensible knowledge is renewed only when the spirit of God opens people to the divine perfection "as manifested in the works he has done, and in the words that he has spoken."[13] For Edwards that comprehension applies not to some exclusively religious compartment of life, but to everything we know.[14] In particular, however, it applies to "Enthusiasm," "Awakenings," "Convictions," and to the literally "sensationalist" preaching he himself practiced. The aim was not to practice right interpretation of Scripture, right sacrament, or right belief, but to bring to the dull and sinful heart a true and vital sense of the "sensational" world in its natural spiritual depths.

This technique of salvation is elaborated in Edwards's "Ideas, Sense of the Heart, Spiritual Knowledge or Conviction. Faith." Perry Miller found this previously unpublished fragment in the Yale archives and published it in the *Harvard Theological Review* in 1948. In his preface accompanying that piece, Miller acknowledges that Edwards "is generally rated an 'idealist' and a 'Puritan Platonist,' " but argues that the "peculiar and fascinating character of his [Edwards's] achievement is entirely lost if he be not seen as the first and most radical, even though the most tragically misunderstood, of American empiricists."[15] Miller goes on to say, "In Edwards' sense of the heart, there is nothing transcendental; it is rather a sensuous apprehension of the total situation."[16] Even more bluntly, Miller adds that, for Edwards, "the spirit of God works through the mechanism of sense impression."[17]

In all this Miller relies on the Lockean connection—that in 1717 the fourteen-year-old Edwards obtained a copy of Locke's *Essay Concerning Human Understanding* and "grasped in a flash" that "Locke was the masterspirit of the age."[18] Miller claims that Edwards then realized that "God's way" is through sensations of this world; it is one of "indirection, which is the only way, because speaking the unspeakable is impossible."[19]

Norman Fiering in *Jonathan Edwards's Moral Thought and Its British Context* rejects what he calls Miller's "dramatic picture of the relationship between Edwards and Locke."[20] While conceding that Edwards was "enormously excited" by Locke's *Essay*, Fiering questions whether the *Essay* was "the central and decisive event in his [Edwards's] intellectual life."[21]

Fiering's larger point is that Edwards in most respects is not an Enlightenment thinker.[22] Fiering, in effect, attacks not only Miller's contention but the general argument that Edwards is an American radical empiricist. Fiering argues that Edwards relied not on empirical evidence but "on moral theology for his conclusions."[23] In fact, Fiering argues that Edwards's moral and spiritual senses "are outright repudiations of Lockean empiricism, not imitations of it."[24] Fiering supports this by noting that Edwards, in a non-Lockean way, looked to divine grace, instead of observable nature, and to the subjective reality of sin, instead of observable vices.[25] If there is a philosophical precedent, says Fiering, it is more likely the Cambridge Platonists than Locke.[26]

Fiering is undoubtedly correct and helpful in demonstrating that Miller's account of Edwards's dependence on Locke is exaggerated, that it may be off-base on several particulars (such as the date of Edwards's first reading of Locke), and that Miller fails properly to account for other possible sources of Edwards's distinctive ideas.[27] Further, if to be a Lockean is to accept Locke's doctrines without qualification, Fiering is correct again, for Edwards did not accept Locke without qualification.

It is on this last point, however, where Fiering's analysis is unfair, for Miller is not simply "the purveyor of the tradition that has emphasized Locke's influence on Edwards,"[28] as Fiering contends. Miller is not concerned to establish that in all respects Edwards was a Lockean, but primarily that in epistemology and in his analysis of language Edwards was a revisionary—not an orthodox—Lockean, and an empiricist, rather than a Platonic idealist. Miller is quite aware, for example, that Edwards's willingness to use words to arouse affections was a violation of Locke's mandate to avoid "Enthusiasm."[29] Further, even within the restricted area of epistemology Miller acknowledges in his 1948 *Harvard Theological Review* article (to which Fiering makes no reference) that Edwards is not an orthodox Lockean, for "Edwards works his way from the Lockean theory of language to his distinction between the 'understanding of the head' and the 'sense of the heart.' "[30] Miller proceeds to demonstrate how the sense of the heart, as it apprehends "the total situation," incorporates more than Locke's natural sensations of nature.

Further, Miller and others who argue for a Lockean influence,[31] do not dismiss, as Fiering suggests, Edwards's concern for "theological" grace and sin, but instead contend that Edwards's revisionary Lockean epistemology is just as attentive to "theological" grace as to material nature, to "theological" sin as to material vices. The genius of Edwards's sense of the heart—as opposed to Locke's five-sense sensationalism—was that it could sensuously perceive grace and sin as well as nature and vice. For Edwards, to be fully sensuous was to be theological.

If epistemology is the issue, Miller's case would seem to hold. Of course, in other areas the case against Edwards being even a revisionary Enlightenment thinker is strong. For example, Edwards's preoccupation with sin and his trust in the crucial importance of God's role in salvation militate against the Enlightenment's movement towards a notion of human autonomy. Even Locke, however, denied human autonomy in religious matters.[32]

Finally, and at the risk of making labored this defense of Edwards as a radical empiricist, I should comment on the relation of this debate about Edwards's epistemology to one aspect of post-modern understandings of history. If we have learned anything from deconstructionist hermeneutics and historicism,[33] we should be skeptical about extended debates about the nature of the author's true intention, debates which assume both that the authorial intention can be ascertained, and that to ascertain it is of the utmost importance. The crucial question is not, then, What did Edwards think of Locke? But, Can Edwards be plausibly interpreted as a radical empiricist, extending Locke's empiri-

cism into a broader American mode? Miller and Fiering betray
their own heavyhandedness in portraying what was to have been
Edwards's own opinion. They have opposite tasks to perform
regarding Edwards's citations of Locke. Miller must explain why,
if Edwards is a revisionary Lockean, he did not cite Locke more
than he did. Fiering must explain why, if Edwards is an anti-
Lockean Platonist, he cited Locke as much as he did. So Miller
opines that Edwards was so intimidated by his tutor's, Samuel
Johnson's, warnings about the prejudices against the "new philosophy" that Edwards had no choice but "to be extremely
cautious about avowing what Locke meant to him."[34] Fiering
speculates in exactly the opposite direction, that Edwards cited
Locke as often as he did only in order to placate the friends of
Locke among his readers: "Edwards circumvented Locke by
borrowing enough of his fashionable language to satisfy empiricist critics."[35] In my own efforts to present Miller's interpretation, I have indulged in a little Millerean speculation—just as I
will speculate about intentions as I discuss other empiricists. My
real argument, however, is that Edwards, whatever his authorial
intention, can be read as a radical empiricist. His writings in
general, and his use of the word "sense" in particular, can be
properly regarded as contributing to a new American empiricism,
building on but moving beyond John Locke's Essay. While I do
not think Edwards's Lockean epistemology was unintentional, I
think it could have been, and the interpretation would remain the
same.

Undoubtedly, if Edwards had been interpreted as a radical
empiricist earlier, his effect on American intellectual history
would have been different. Perry Miller jumps the 150 years
from Edwards's death to William James's radical empirical writings, and acknowledges that the failure to see Edwards as an
empiricist has had its effects. Miller speculates that had
Edwards's fragment, published in 1948 in the Harvard Theological Review, been published instead in the 1790s, then James
would have had "a mighty American precedent for his stand
against both psychological atomism and transcendental categories."[36] In the intervening years in philosophy, the demand for
clarity had increased, the preoccupation with the thing-in-itself

had increased, and the plausibility of the sense relation between the self and a physically real empirical object had decreased. James, however, returned to Locke, attacked both transcendental idealism and deterministic positivism, and enunciated what he thought was a new empiricism. He called it "radical empiricism," but it was in large part an unwitting resumption of a direction already implicit in Edwards's own epistemology.

James's empiricism was, however, newly explicit in grounding truth only on what is physically experienced and in affirming that relations are experienced just as surely as atomic things are. For James, it was in those relations that real worth was sensed. He was empirically orthodox in his rejection of transempirical ideas; he was empirically unorthodox in his claim that some of the values which idealists hoped to justify speculatively are, in fact, discerned empirically. He was empirically orthodox in recognizing evidence for "bare activity," or for that sheer fact of eventfulness; he was empirically unorthodox in recognizing that activity comes to the observer "with definite direction; it comes with desire and sense of goal; it comes complicated with resistances which it overcomes or succumbs to."[37] James went on to argue that, when one opposes or collaborates with these valuational complications, they are felt empirically, just as "loud," "red," or "sweet" are felt empirically by one experiencing them.[38] Stated more specifically, in the objective, physical world there are "affective phenomena" and "appreciative attributes of things, their dangerousness, beauty, rarity, utility, etc."; and such "emphases" in objects, when the subject opposes or collaborates with them, induce "bodily effects upon us, alterations of tone and tension, of heartbeat and breathing, of vascular and visceral action."[39] And when felt with particular attentiveness, these effects are brought to consciousness and often termed values.

For James, religious worth is sensed in a comparable way. We do experience an objective wrongness in ourselves, but we also do experience a "more," a "wider self," which, when we make ourselves continuous with it, can to some extent save us from that wrongness.[40] James's Varieties of Religious Experience illustrates the varieties of the religious sense of the "more." For sheer voluptuousness James's accounts may fall short of Edwards's own testimony to "a calm, sweet, cast, or appearance of divine glory" in the sun, moon, stars, sky, grass, flowers, trees, and "all nature."[41] But James did contribute a new empirical plausibility to the claim that there are religious—and yet, physical—intuitions which "come from a deeper level of your nature than the loquacious level which rationalism inhabits."[42]

Like Edwards and James, Alfred North Whitehead reverts particularly to John Locke's *Essay*, and generally to "that phase of philosophic thought which began with Descartes and ended with Hume."[43] Unlike Edwards and James, Whitehead argues that all creatures, not only humans, affectively experience the worth of the world.

For Whitehead "each pulsation of actuality" or "existence in its own nature,"[44] begins as an experience of value. The sheer casual efficacy of the past world on the present subject "is emotional—blind emotion—received as felt elsewhere in another occasion and conformally appropriated as a subjective passion."[45] The subject, in turn, dimly evaluates this encountered emotional value and, usually primitively and nonconsciously, decides to reject or accept it.

For Edwards and James the sense of value is confined to human experience. Despite the fact that for Edwards the sense of value can refer to nature, so that nature contains value, only humans can experience value, because value experience is affectional and only humans have affections. At this point Edwards sounds very Platonic; only humans have minds, and the mind, not the body, "is the proper seat of affections."[46] While James, an anti-Platonic, mind-body monist, did contend that all experience begins physically (so that the body is the seat of the affections), he also claimed that the only bodily experience which leads to the experience of values is found in "that part of physical nature which our own skin covers."[47] So, said James, to imagine that nonhumans can experience value is to be the victim of a mere "anthropomorphic projection."

Whitehead's argument that all creatures affectively experience the worth of the world distinguishes his doctrine of God from that of Edwards and James. To the extent that Edwards's and James's God is tied to human experience, it will effectively die with the human race and as a source of value remain forever meaningless, as it is now for nonhumans. For Whitehead, on the other hand, value is not only universally experienced, but by its universal availability gives to the world an organic unity. It is our sense of the presence of value everywhere in the world which lies at the bottom of our "intuition of holiness, the intuition of the sacred, which is the foundation of all religion."[48]

Whitehead's panpsychic scope of value stakes out the full boundaries of radical empiricism. Succeeding radical empiricists are left with the task of erecting the forms and uses of radical empiricism.

Our fourth radical empiricist philosopher, John Dewey, set forth his radical empiricism most adequately in the opening chapter of his *Experience and Nature*. And here he too traced the epistemological problems of dualism and intellectualism primarily to Descartes, Locke and Hume.

In *Art as Experience* Dewey claims that art, as a type of experience, begins when a moment of experience has sufficient unity to make it into "an experience." "An experience" has a "thatness," a single "quality" which distinguishes it from all other experience. While this quality is subjective, it receives its intellectual and emotional aspects from the experienced environment. The radicalness of Dewey's empiricism lies in his insistence that the emotional aspect is based on a sense of the objective world. He says, "The live animal does not have to project emotions into the objects experienced. Nature is kind and hateful, bland and morose, irritating and comforting, long before she is mathematically qualified or even a cogeries of 'secondary' qualities like colors and their shapes."[49] The emotional sense feels the environment so immediately that it is best described as a largely nonconscious and certainly noncognitive intuition. Finally, Dewey uses the word "mystical" to describe the intuition at its greatest intensity. The mystical intuition reaches for the ever broader quality of the "whole," the most universal bounds of that which is experienced. Art, in particular, can suggest that wholeness in such a way that we can have "the religious feeling that accompanies intense aesthetic perception. We are, as it were, introduced into a world beyond this world which is nevertheless the deeper reality of the world in which we live our ordinary experience."[50]

It is my contention that the empiricism set forth by these thinkers is a new and American epistemology. As a movement radical empiricism is unique to America, but as a doctrine radical empiricism is enunciated by certain persons beyond the borders of the United States—most notably Henri Bergson. Particularly in his *Creative Evolution* Bergson worked out of a naturalistic empiricism and added to the five senses a sense of intuition, or sympathy, which was in its own way a sense of value. Both James and Whitehead openly acknowledged their debt to Bergson, and the biological orientation of his radical empiricism is distinctive even today.

In America radical empiricism, like a local germ, had passed from Edwards, had almost died, but had been kept alive in the lungs of many of the eighteenth and nineteenth century American clergy; it had been caught by James and then propagated most infectiously by Dewey in the 1920s and 1930s. But when American philosophy took a positivistic and then a linguistic turn, radical empiricism's most congenial host again may have been theological. Radical empiricism was implicit in the socio-historical method of members of the Chicago School of theology, particularly in the work of Shailer Mathews and Shirley Jackson Case in the first five decades of this century. Radical empiricism was explicit in the empirical work of several empirical process theologians, particularly Henry Nelson Wieman, Bernard Meland, and Bernard Loomer, from the 1920s to the 1970s.

These last three add to American radical empiricism a sustained consideration of the religious sense of value. Although each theologian in his own way is quite complex and draws from a variety of sources, each theologian's radical empiricism can be analyzed by showing how it is related to the thought of a philosophical predecessor: Henry Nelson Wieman's empiricism to Dewey's thought;[51] Bernard Meland's empiricism to James's thought; Bernard Loomer's empiricism to Whitehead's thought.

Henry Nelson Wieman usually argues for a radically empirical sense of value. Occasionally he will dismiss the testimony of the sense of value if it cannot be confirmed by reference to objective consequences observable by the five senses. However, when Bernard Meland charged that Wieman's radical empiricism was weak, Wieman virtually replicated Dewey's notion of the unique "quality" of an experience. Wieman denied that distinct sense experience, such as the green color of the tree, could specify the nonsensuous and "unique experience of the moment" with the tree.[52] Further, he says, "these fleeting qualities of sense and feeling, which elude all description and hence all cognition, are no more subjective than the structures which we apply to them by specifying time, place, size, weight, direction, number of elements, and all the other forms used in knowledge."[53] Wieman claims that "the tragedy of man and his generic sin is to try to put all existence into servitude of specifiable structures of truth,"[54] for these are merely a "thin layer of oil" over the ocean of the "infinitely complex structure of events composing this vast society of interacting organisms and their sustaining or destructive environment."[55] Wieman warns the reader that his typical concentration on the specifiable structures is a mere accident of his scholarly objectives.[56]

This radicalness of Wieman's empiricism applies also to religious experience where "we confront and accept the immediate deliverance of all our sensitivity; we expose ourselves most completely to the impact of fact in its rawest and most massive form."[57] The religious attitude involves the "mergence of the individual with the total movement of all things."[58] Wieman will call this attitude a "mystic consciousness" and claim that "worship at its best is precisely this."[59]

At the same time, however, like the Dewey of A Common Faith, Wieman will argue that this mystic consciousness is "misused" if it is not used also to generate new and practical meanings;[60] he will contend that to dwell on the awarenesss of the divine depth by itself, apart from any instrumental use in practical living, is a positive "evil."[61]

Bernard Meland interprets Wieman's insistence on use as a reduction of "immediate awareness to tested knowledge"[62] and argues that Dewey's instrumentalism "led back into the trail of positivism."[63] While Meland's characterization of Wieman and

Dewey may overemphasize one side of these men and neglect the other, they do indicate Meland's sensitivity to the fact that radical empiricism is a distinct and easily perverted orientation of thought.

The empirical appreciation of value, says Meland, derives from the objective structure of a society's experience as that exists in scriptures, in churches, and in all the artistic, economic, social and idiomatic gestures of a culture. It is felt initially as a largely nonconscious and certainly noncognitive "wisdom of the body." Any effort to ignore or censure aspects of that experience is, for Meland, not only blasphemous, but demented.[64] The ultimacy, or "Creative Passage," implicit in that structure of experience is felt with an "appreciate awareness" as "a good not our own." It is blatantly contradictory, therefore, to exclude every component of that "good not our own" except what we can certify as thoroughly intelligible, and in that sense as a good which is our own.[65]

In spirit, Meland's efforts are closer to James's thought than to that of any other philosopher. Not only does Meland cite James's work as "the most impressive justification for sensitive awareness in thought which is to be found either in philosophical or psychological literature,"[66] but in his own work Meland follows James's lead in avoiding pragmatic, positivistic, or rationalistic simplifications of the complex deliverances of the sense of depth. Meland's radical empiricism is studiously universal in its openness. He strives for a consistency of appreciation, exclusive of nothing except premature closure, inclusive of everything which might regard human awareness. In this he moves further than any American except, possibly, Bernard Loomer.

In the early 1970s Bernard Loomer began to introduce what may be an additional step in a radically empirical theological awareness. It is inspired by an empirical tenacity which takes a cue from Whitehead. "Suffice it to say," says Loomer, "that I am attempting to do theologically what Whitehead suggested should be done philosophically, namely, to take a set of ideas, the best that one has, and unflinchingly to explore experience with the aid of those ideas."[67] Loomer's empiricism moves beyond Meland's in this way: the empirical limit in theological knowledge leaves Meland without real evidence that what is ultimate is supremely powerful, but it leaves Loomer without any real evidence that what is ultimate is either supremely powerful or supremely good.[68]

Loomer's argument appears in its fullest form in his essay, "The Size of God," but is anticipated in several articles written in the 1970s.[69] In "The Size of God" Loomer holds that "physical feelings are the fundamental avenues through which we meet and absorb the elemental forces of our existence," and that through these feelings we experience "the effective and evaluative dimensions of life."[70] The genius of his argument is to hue exactly to the line extending from this epistemological premise. If physical feelings are fundamental, then all abstractions are derivative and partial. Therefore, if we are to know holistically, we must stick with physical feelings and the concreteness they apprehend. Consequently, our knowledge of God must be derived from physical feelings. Because physical feelings indicate a world which is valuationally ambiguous, we have no choice but to accept the valuational ambiguity of God and to reject all traditional doctrines which hold that God is unambiguous or perfect, for they make of God an abstraction rather than a concrete reality. As known only empirically, God fosters greater evil as well as greater good; and, doing this, God is "the organic restlessness of the whole body of creation."[71]

Loomer designates "size" as the name for the aesthetic ideal which still stands after this empiricist onslaught. Size is the capacity aesthetically to incorporate as much diversity of physical feelings as one can without losing one's own identity. Loomer's empiricism prizes the size not only of the creature, but of God, who integrates the diverse movements toward both evil and good. Loomer claims to find empirically the divine ambiguity and thus, the divine size (or stature) missed by Wieman and Whitehead, who through abstractions insisted on the unambiguous goodness of God. Ironically, God's ambiguity, God's participation in both good and evil, permits God's size; and this leads Loomer unambiguously to associate God with aesthetic perfection—a perfection which is never a simple harmony, and which is always emerging and always riddled with the dissonant combination of real loss and real gain.

Here then is one possible line of thinkers (others could have been chosen) who corporately enunciated a uniquely American empiricism, with both philosophical and theological applications. The efforts to describe a "sense of the heart" (Edwards), "bodily effects" (James), "causal efficacy" (Whitehead), and a sense of "quality" (Dewey) comprised a movement of thought unanticipated and unduplicated by any other corporate philosophical endeavor. The efforts to theologically realize this empiricism in Wieman's idea of experience beyond specification, in Meland's "appreciative awareness" and in Loomer's sense of "size" yielded a distinctively empirical process theology.

However, even though empirical process theology did occupy a propitious place in American intellectual history, it was not accorded much attention by academic theologians. Those theologians who possessed a post-liberal sensibility and who were inclined to take seriously process theology's general picture, tended to gravitate more readily to a rationalistic form of process theology, principally that of Charles Hartshorne and of his leading exponents, Schubert Ogden and (the early) John Cobb, Jr. Consequently, rationalistic process theology not only rivaled, but partially eclipsed empirical process theology.

Hartshorne in 1941 wrote *Man's Vision of God* and in 1943 within the University of Chicago moved from a full-time commitment in the Department of Philosophy to a joint appointment between the Department of Philosophy and the Divinity School. He believed that his work accepted the mandate of radical empiricism, but added to it the empirical rationalism of Charles Sanders Peirce together with an amplification of Whitehead's rationalism, particularly as that is found in *Process and Reality*. Hartshorne argued that to treat empiricism and rationalism as mutually exclusive ways of knowing is to be unnecessarily simple; it is to indulge in an illegitimate "favoritism."[72] It makes more sense, Hartshorne argued, to include both, using empiricism to know God in its relativity and rationalism to know God in its absoluteness. In his own writing, however, Hartshorne concentrated on the rationalistic knowledge of God in its absoluteness, a knowledge based largely on the a priori speculation which flowed from what everyone must mean by "perfection" as it is applied to God. In *Man's Vision of God* (1941) and *The Divine Relativity* (1948) Hartshorne initiated a rationalistic process philosophy of religion which soon drew far greater attention than that drawn by empirical process theology.

However, from the standpoint of radical empiricism, Hartshorne's rationalistic process theology can be confusing. It seems to reject just those limits empiricism imposes on knowledge. Hartshorne's augmentation of radical empiricism by rationalism seems analogous to Kierkegaard's deciding to become a Hegelian too. Radical empiricism, historically understood, is among other things a revolt against rationalism. It is a studious effort not to be empirical in part but to be totally empirical—that is, to be empirical without introducing any nonempirical or a priori contents, even when including such contents might provide a more satisfying completeness to one's system, even when excluding such contents might leave one with a most unsatisfying and painful obscurity.[73]

Admittedly, Hartshorne's empiricism, as far as it goes, appears to be compatible with empirical process theology. In his *A Natural Theology for Our Time* Hartshorne argues that God in our particular past can be known only confessionally and empirically. But then, a page later, Hartshorne claims that such empirical knowledge is intelligible only if rationalist knowledge is also intelligible ("surpassable modes of interaction are intelligible only if unsurpassable ways are also intelligible").[74] It is this introduction of rationalistic ways of knowing which is confusing from the standpoint of radical empiricism.

The empiricism of some of Hartshorne's students, as far as that goes, also appears to be compatible with radical empiricism. Schubert Ogden, for example, has written a classic exposition of the theological implications of Whitehead's empiricism.[75] Ogden's rationalism, however, leads him to affirm that none of us who acts on moral grounds can accept "the eventual nullity of his decisions" nor can we who act on moral grounds finally deny "the abiding worth of our life."[76] Ogden's argument about the infinite future (the abidingness of our life's worth) appears to be without empirical warrant—as does Ogden's claim that God is "the necessary condition of our existence as selves" and that God has a dipolar nature.[77]

In short, while empirical process theology clearly belongs to the history of American religious empiricism, rationalistic process theology's relation to that tradition is ambiguous.

A More Viable American Theology

Radical empiricist philosophers distinguished themselves from eighteenth century British empiricists by adding to the five senses certain other senses, such as the sense of beauty, the sense of a "more," the senses of aversion or attraction, and the senses of quality. Further, these philosophers claimed that these valuational senses had an objective referent, that they responded to a locus of objective value in the world. However, in their writings they did not develop the possibility that human history, itself, might constitute their own best objective source of values. They accepted the valuational content which only history contains, yet they never undertook a disciplined examination of the events of history, except the history of philosophy. Neither did the radical empiricist philosophers establish a disciplined method of historical analysis. In their discussion of the moral, aesthetic, or even religious values which might underlie history, they never enunciated a method whereby those values might be empirically sensed in and induced from specific historical phenomena.

Like the radical empiricist philosophers, the empirical process theologians failed to undertake any specific studies of historical events, or even to formulate an explicit philosophy of history, despite the fact that they had the added impetus which comes from working within the Judeo-Christian tradition—for which the sense of history is central. From the writers of the Pentateuch, through the historians of the kingdoms of Israel, through the prophets and wisdom writers, through the authors of the gospels and epistles, through the church historians and the biblical and historical theologians of the Christian community, it had been assumed that God acted in the social histories of the Israelites and the Christians. The Jewish and Christian faiths tended to come to this: either our history bears evidence of the working of God or we are lost. Nevertheless, the challenge to study historical events for what they might indicate religiously was never quite accepted by the empirical process theologians.

They did begin to work toward developing a religious sense of history in one respect: they applied their conclusion about God to experiences which assumed regular patterns. Wieman applied his conclusions about God to regularities in the natural process, and Loomer applied his conclusions about God to apparent regularities in human conduct.

In particular, Meland applied his conclusions about God to apparent regularities in culture. He said that theologians should attempt to read the underlying mythos out of historical experience, and that when they did this they were undertaking "constructive theology"—that theology concerned with perceiving the realities of faith in the immediacies of experience.[78] Meland's *The Seeds of Redemption* and *The Reawakening of the Christian Faith* described the specific and new ills endemic to the contemporary era and postulated what the new divine response to those ills might be. Meland's empiricism has always sought the social meaning of the realities of faith; he broke down the process structures of thought by running them through the sieve of cultural anthropology and the history of religions. However, no matter to what extent he recognized that contemporary culture must be historically understood, he did not, I believe, move beyond a rather impressionistic interpretation of any culture and of what God might be revealing through cultures. Meland's main point, again, was and is that we must know God as making such a revelation; but this itself is an essentially epistemological point. While Meland more than anyone has advanced the historical discussion, he did not undertake specific analysis of religious phenomena.

Meland and the other empirical process theologians, if they were really to assess experience empirically, needed a method of reading history. But a method of history they did not have. Meland did acknowledge that not only his predecessors among the radical empiricists, but he himself failed "to articulate the primal flux of immediacy in ways that would present it as something more compelling than an ambiguous, preconscious flux, awaiting conceptualization." "There still is lacking in my procedure," Meland said, "both a methodical way of focusing these occurrences of religious inquiry, and a method of inquiry suitable to the task of probing their theological import."[79]

In effect, empirical process theologians walked to the door of history, but did not take the next and logical step—into a disciplined interpretation of biblical and post-biblical religious histories and into a disciplined interpretation of what might be termed the presence or effects of the divine in those histories. While these theologians continued to use God language, they never developed pragmatic tests for what empirical difference God might make—admittedly, tests unimaginable by present standards. Nevertheless, this is crucially important because the signal contributions of these theologians to the doctrine of God is the notion that the living God is a God who changes, who, as concrete, is always new and, ostensibly, would create new influences. It is that specificity of God's action in history which is alone real. On empirical grounds there is no such thing as abstract knowledge; there is only concrete, particular knowledge, which might be generalized about. If God's novel and concrete actions are to be read, they must be read empirically, out of specific historical situations or out of individuals' historically situated modes of experiencing. And yet, such historical readings were not accomplished, nor was a specific method for that reading derived by empirical process theologians.

This is all the more ironic in view of the fact that the empirical process theologians were the successors to earlier Chicago School empirical theologians for whom history was not only a central category in principle, but also the central object of actual inquiry. For Chicago scholars such as Shailer Mathews and Shirley Jackson Case, biblical and ecclesiastical histories were the principal object of research. They were not particularly self-conscious about their epistemology, and did not deliberately address and attempt to develop the theological uses of the radical empiricism so important to the empirical process theologians. Mathews's and Case's socio-historical method was, however, an important moment in American religious empiricism. Nevertheless, their historical emphasis has been largely lost on the empirical process theologians who succeeded them at Chicago.

Now it should be recognized that philosophers and philosophical theologians have seldom ever dedicated themselves to careful, historical inquiry. They are legitimately preoccupied with the initial questions of epistemology, metaphysics, methodology, ethics, and aesthetics, leaving the induction from specific historical contents to others. Further, we can hardly imagine what it would mean to undertake such induction, particularly given the enormous experiential and historical complexity allowed by the empirical process theologians. Yet the question still hangs.

That question, however, may be clarified through reopening the issue of historical method, particularly as it has been reconceived in the historicism of certain, post-modernists, such as Jacques Derrida and John Wheeler.

Chapter 2

An Historicist Interpretation: The Deconstruction and Reconstruction of Religious Knowledge

Whatever order there is in our world, be it rational, ethical, or aesthetic, derives from the interconnectedness of things, not the other way round.[1]

In American religious empiricism the only authority is experience; and for that empiricism all theological construction is free construction by experience on experience. It is construction by the present on the felt past, by the interpretive side of experience on the receptive side of experience. It is free, rather than bound by an unchanging norm, because it is a construction which reinterprets what it receives from the past. Yet it is constrained rather than completely arbitrary, because it is a construction on—based on and limited by—what is inherited from the past.

This commentary on construction is elementary, at least for those empirical theologians working out of the process philosophies of William James, John Dewey, and, especially, Alfred North Whitehead. What is not elementary is what, in such a processive context, history is and how history is known. On this question rest the present religious authority and meaning of the

41

Bible, of the historic church, and of recent historic events. Either religious empiricism shows how it tests, corroborates, or verifies its conclusions from history, or its conclusions are largely unjustified. It cannot rationally or spiritually intuit a historical order out of some eternal logos or divine will. It must look to the near chaos of history itself and out of this alone ascertain an order; and it must say how that order is religiously meaningful. But most important, it must say how an objective religious order can be generated at all in the ever-moving flow of history.

The need for a concept of history is central to empirical theology the way it is not for other theologies. For example, more rationalistic theologies, such as Charles Hartshorne's, seek to know God largely through the use of a priori reason; and as a consequence, they depend less on what is learned a posteriori, from history, than does religious empiricism. Stated positively, American religious empiricists are entirely adrift in the always evolving interconnections of historical process and in the empirical knowledge that historical process makes possible. So, for them, it is crucial to discern a religious (or moral or aesthetic) contour in history. They must admit, with Bernard Loomer, that "whatever order there is in our world, be it rational, ethical, or aesthetic, derives from the interconnectedness of things, not the other way round." The question is, how is it derived? And then, how do we know it?

The recent ideas of two persons, a French philosopher and an American physicist, might suggest to religious empiricism a relevant notion of how historical orders and meanings are derived and known. I refer to Jacques Derrida, the founder of deconstructionism, and to John Wheeler, who could be called the leading deconstructionist in physics. I am not aware that either Derrida or Wheeler have studied the American empirical philosophers and theologians, but they do seem to share with them an empirical and processive vision, and I believe Derrida's and Wheeler's conclusions can contribute to a notion of religious history for religious empiricism.

My discussion of these two persons is specific in two ways. First, I treat the philosophers and theologians just cited very selectively. I concentrate on the two deconstructionist thinkers only at a length sufficient to indicate how they suggest a notion of history. I examine American religious empiricism largely by implication, through a comment on Alfred North Whitehead; and I comment on Whitehead only at a length sufficient to note that his work can accommodate the notion of history suggested by the deconstructionists. Second, at the chapter's end I propose a deconstructionist notion of religious history appropriate to American religious empiricism. The proposal's derivation from the thinkers treated earlier in the chapter is never more than implicit, although the dependence is real.

Derida and the Deconstruction of Social History

In the 1960s Derrida elevated the complexities of reading and writing to what Paul de Man quaintly calls "the dignity of a philosophical question."[2]

For Derrida, writing stands in direct contrast to a particular kind of speaking. To speak is to mirror the logos, to exercise that mode of Western ontological and theological expression that stretches from Plato, through and beyond Hegel, to the present. "Speaking," to use another metaphor, is the name for the onto-theological claim that human discourse can be transparent to eternal Being, known directly through the human spirit and vented immediately through the human voice. "Writing" is Derrida's term for a nonimmediate and explicitly interpretive response to the world. Writing assumes that there is no know-able logos and, hence, never claims to replicate the logos. When writing replaces speaking, a logos-centered, or logocentric, inter-pretation is deconstructed. Writing is a signifier that refers always and only to another sign, and in this reference it is openly and deliberately interpretive—that is, writing's signifier explicitly differs from its signified. The analysis of writing is the analysis of a pluridimensional and diachronic series of significations; it is accomplished by showing how each instance of writing derives from other instances of writing, which in turn derives from other instances of writing. This analysis demonstrates that every writing supplements that about which it writes, which in turn has supplemented that about which it writes, which in turn has supplemented that about which it writes, and on and on. There is no stable center that itself gives meaning to expression. Remaining is play, the interpretive activity freed of the constriction that arises from a belief in the controlling presence of Being.[3]

Derrida's notion of writing implies a notion of the writing and reading of history. History, as the linguistic exercise of the historian, should be composed of sequences of interpretive gestures; it should be writing and not speech. Just as the logocentric constructions of speech generally must be deconstructed, freed of the pretense of logos-centeredness, so historical speech particularly must be deconstructed. If the historian's work were merely a form of speech, historical events themselves would add no meaning: if the historian's words only mirrored the eternal logos shining through historical events, the historical events themselves would be understood to add nothing to reality, for they would be seen as mere copies of the eternal logos.[4] Properly, the historian's writing should be to some extent free and interpretive rather than ostensibly imitative; and it should regard the historical event not as a logos-mirror but as a creative text.

Derrida's theory of writing suggests, then, not only a deconstructed historical writing in words but a deconstructed historical writing in the human activities that compose the historical object. The historical event itself should be seen as a sign, a partially free and interpretive response to what had preceded it in space and time.

To use the word "writing" to refer to all verbal and physical human behavior except speaking is to use the word in a perfectly Derridean way for Derrida uses "writing" to indicate any interpretive human gesture, whether in the arts, politics, or warfare.[5] Consequently, to write history with words is the interpretive gesture responding to whatever "text" precedes it.

To read history, then, is simply to read a "textual chain, the structure of substitution." It is to recognize "that there is nothing outside the text,"[6] that "there has never been anything but writing; there have never been anything but supplements, substitutive significations which could only come forth in a chain of differential references. . . . And thus to infinity. . . ."[7] History, then, is not a "symbol"[8] of eternal Being; and to those for whom history is thought to be such a symbol, Derrida's history would seem to exist in an "abyss."[9]

Even if to write history is to add the process of writing, to supplement the previous supplementations, to newly interpret the old interpretations, to add a difference to a sequence of differences, still, it is not to make a totally free and arbitrary gesture. This would give primacy to the signifier. Illogically, it would entitle the signifier to precede the signified, so that the " 'signifying' signifier would no longer have a possible signified."[10] Rather, the signifier is always to some extent a function of the signified, the subject always to some extent a function of the writing that precedes the subject.[11] Consequently, Derrida urges the importance of "all the instruments of traditional criticism" that work within the limits prescribed by the givenness of the text.[12] Thus, one's free interpretation of history would work within objective limits. "If," says Derrida, "words and concepts receive meaning only in sequences of differences, one can justify one's language, and one's choice of terms, only within a topic [an orientation in space] and an historical strategy."[13]

In short, to write or to read history is to put an interpretation on the historical past, where the historical past itself is understood as nothing other than the pluridimensional and temporal sequences of human interpretations of human interpretations. If writing is understood as the responsive act, then historical writing is about historical writing, which is about historical writing—always understood as both verbal and physical behavior. History has no center beyond itself, for "there is nothing outside the text."[14]

This account of Derrida's historicism has proceeded as though he were not an extremely controversial thinker. In fact, deconstructionist methods of literary criticism have split many university literature departments and prompted anti-deconstructionists to bring their case to the public.[15] Derrida has been attacked as one who would destroy the meaning of discourse. M.H. Abrams objects that "Derrida puts out of play, before the game even begins, every source of norms, controls, or indicators which, in the ordinary use of language, set a limit to what we can mean and what we can be understood to mean."[16] The author and the syntax of the given language are denied all authority, Abrams complains. E. D. Hirsch, Jr.'s *The Aims of Interpretation* is a sustained outcry against what Hirsch sees as the crime of Martin Heidegger and Jacques Derrida: that they have stolen the author's right to give the text an objective meaning.[17] But if the objective meaning of the text is gone, the text is meaningless—or, to say the same thing, the meaning of the text is simply invented in the subjectivity of the reader.

These criticisms of Derrida as a sheer subjectivist neglect the historicity of Derrida's approach. Frank Lentricchia in his *After the New Criticism* offers an historicist analysis of contemporary literary criticism and defends Derrida's general approach. Hirsch misses the historicity in Heidegger and, by implication, in Derrida because, Lentricchia says, Hirsch is misled by his own Cartesian dualism. Lentricchia argues that "the basic charge, that Heidegger and his followers are solipsistic relativists, stems from a traditional conception of the subject-object model which delegates the subject *qua* subject to the privacy of its perspectives."[18]

Hirsch's and Abrams's attacks on Derrida might best be viewed as a consequence of the modernist point of view. The assumption lying behind that point of view is, in Descartes's words, that "thought is an attribute that belongs to me; it alone is inseparable from my nature."[19] This, in turn, leads to what might be called the modernist's predicament: How can this "me" know the world outside itself? Descartes's self-world dualism, particularly as it is developed by Locke, Hume, and Kant, assumes that the self and the world are distinguishable and isolatable from each other; this, in turn, makes the primary philosophical problem the epistemological problem of how the self can gain contact with and know the world. From the modernist standpoint Derrida is the worst conceivable threat, for he has denied the authority of the logos, the author, or the book; this means that the objective world, as it is, cannot penetrate the subjectivity of the knower, leaving the isolatable self trapped in solipsistic ignorance.

Lentricchia's objection to this can be described in terms of the fallacy of the excluded middle. Many of the critics of Derrida fear that if the objective world, in its objectivity, cannot be transported into the mind of the knower, then the knower will be forever blind. Lentricchia's response, in effect, is to install a third option, the historicist option, which can be used only if a Cartesian dualism is abandoned. The historicist option is found in Derrida's project of tracing what Lentricchia calls the "ineffaceable historicity of discourse,"[20] for in this project there is the "implication of a postructuralist historical method that would yield a positive kind of knowledge."[21] Lentricchia acknowledges that at times Derrida neglects his own historicism.[22] But when he is faithful to it, Derrida follows Heidegger, who Lentricchia says never accepted the Cartesian dualism out of which Hirsch and most other critics of derrida work. Heidegger never speaks of the isolated subject *qua* subject. For Heidegger human reality as *Dasein* discloses "transpersonal and transcultural existential modes."[23] In other words, the self for Heidegger is not finally distinguishable from nor separable from the other; to know the self is to know history, and vice versa. This historicist view of the inseparability of the self and the world suggests a third form of knowledge, neither objectivist nor subjectivist, but historicist.

Applied to Derrida, this means that to speak of the subject is to speak of the object, to speak of the signifier is to speak of the signified. The either-or does not apply; to deny that the object can be known in its purity is not to force the solipsistic alternative. For to know the object as known by the subject is still to know the object, even if not in its objective purity. Conversely, to know something of the chain of interpretations is to know something of the subject regarding that chain.

This historicist option seems lost on the otherwise deeply insightful Yale Derrideans, J. Hillis Miller, Paul de Man, and Geoffrey Hartman, as they apply Derrida's deconstructionism to literary critical theory and practice. Although they defend Derrida, they seem content, Lentricchia says, "to spread terror in traditionalist quarters."[24] The Yale Derrideans have extended Derrida's deconstructionism to a deconstruction of all referentiality. The Yale School, allows the critic alone, rather than the critic in combination with the objective mandate of the literary work, to determine the meaning of the literary work. This gives clear primacy to the subject, making the Yale critics perfect illustrations of what Hirsch has feared, and allowing them to neglect Derrida's historicism. A major consequence is that the deconstructionist project often is presented to literature departments as authentically nihilistic.[25]

There are indications that much the same neglect of Derrida's historicism will be repeated by an otherwise very important group of theological Derrideans. Principal among them are Carl Raschke, Charles Winquist, Mark C. Taylor, and Thomas Altizer, as they write in *Deconstruction and Theology*. Mark Taylor's own *Deconstructing Theology* makes adventurous preliminary moves, but his *Erring: A Postmodern A/theology* is the most complete application of deconstruction to theology yet written.[26] Together, these theologians contribute appreciably to the task of bringing theology into the late twentieth century. But, finally, they render deconstruction so subjectivistically and so formalistically that there is little positive meaning left either to religious history or to God. In Winquist's words, "God can be created semantically through metaphorical gain."[27] Carl Raschke assumes (unnecessarily) that theology to be theology must be logocentric. Hence, he thinks of deconstruction as the self-destruction of a theology which realizes that logocentrism is no longer sustainable. Deconstruction in theology, then, simply reveals "the inherent nihilism of its host discipline. Where the body is there shall the eagles gather."[28]

Derrida's historicism is congenial to the empirical philosophies of James, Dewey, and Whitehead. In fact, these empirical philosophers and their theological protegees offer to Derrida a cosmological foundation, one which is more cognizant of the developments in the sciences than the historicism of Heidegger or the historicism of Michel Foucault, both of whom Lentricchia champions as sources of a new philosophical historicism. These American empiricists all reject the Cartesian duality between the isolatable self and the isolatable world; they all begin with the assumption that the self is, in one way or another, comprised of its relations with the world. They all deny that there is any human substance or essence which is what it is apart from its relations with the world. To paraphrase Whitehead, the notion of creativity is a picture of the many of the world becoming the one which is the subject, so that the many of the world is, in turn, increased by one.[29]

This American empiricist cosmology is an historicist cosmology because it sees the self as an expression of history. The middle option, excluded by the modernist tradition, is gained by the philosophers and theologians of process through an emphasis on relatedness, or through seeing the subject as internally related to the object. Whitehead's "principle of relativity" states the matter in what may seem to be an extreme way by claiming that every object in the universe is involved in the development of each subject.[30] The historicist implication is inescapable: if the subject is what it is largely because of its history, then to know the subject is to know not an isolated being, but to know an objective history from one angle.

For James and Dewey the historian's writing would be built from experiences, and experiences are composed of relations with the past as interpreted from the standpoint of and, to some extent, with the freedom of the interpreting subject. Most of what Whitehead wrote in the 1920s and 1930s, particularly his *Symbolism: Its Meaning and Effect* and *Modes of Thought*, calls for the same priority of experience and implies the same nonlogocentric estimate of the historian's writing. (Admittedly, Whitehead's notions of speculative reason, of the initial aim, and of the conceptual reversion from the primordial nature of God, as they are described in *The Function of Reason*, in *Process and Reality*, and in *Religion in the Making*, are logocentric notions; this rationalistic side of Whitehead will not be considered in what follows.)

Further, for James and Dewey, and for Whitehead (with the exceptions just noted), not only the words of the historian but also the historical object compose a nonlogocentric, interpretive, or freely constructive form of historical writing. For the historical object, whether human or nonhuman, once was a subject receiving and interpreting its past, rather than mirroring an eternal logos.[31]

In these ways, then, James's, Dewey's, and Whitehead's works and, in effect, the empirical theology grounded on these works all contain the elements for a notion of historical development that is consistent with Derrida's. There remains, however, between American works and those of Derrida a difference that must be addressed if a notion of historical order adequate to empirical process theology is to be developed.

For Derrida the object of deconstructive interpretation is only human behavior, whereas for the American empiricist, and for the empirical theologian as well, all events, both human behavior and events of nature, must be the objects of deconstructive interpretations. Derrida's ideas, although they may move beyond the subject-object dualism of his critics, still appear to be imbued with a Kantian dualism of world and self, a dualism between fact and value, nature and human history, causally determined matter and freely developed meanings, scientific studies and human studies. The first member of the pair, the question of nature, is neglected, presumably given over to science. For Derrida, the second member of the pair, the question of human history, alone constitutes the arena for deconstructionist activity. Here is found free, human, meaningful behavior, here logocentrism is ruled out, and here alone are found the phenomena of psychology, anthropology, philosophy, semiotics, art, politics, and, possibly, even religion to which deconstructionist interpretation can be properly applied. This is all reminiscent of earlier neo-Kantians, such as Dilthey, who focused on *Verstandnis*, and Bultmann, who concerned himself primarily with the meaning of *Geschichte*. They have concentrated their hermeneutical work on what Kant called reason in its practical aspect as against reason in its pure aspect. Equally, the theologians writing in *Deconstruction and Theology* (Raschke, Winquist, Taylor, Altizer, Robert Scharlemann, and Max Myers) in their use of Derrida, Freud, Heidegger, Nietzsche, Hegel, and other Continental thinkers bifurcate the world and ignore nature.

By contrast, the empiricism of Whitehead, James, and Dewey and of American empirical theologians is polemically antibifurcated, explicit in its advocacy of a nature-history or self-world continuum. In its elevation of that single reality that is experience, it collapses the dualisms of spirit and matter, of the human and the nonhuman. Consequently, a notion of historical order appropriate to American religious empiricism must move beyond Derrida to deconstruct natural history, as well as the social history of human behavior. The development of a deconstruction of science, as it interprets nature, has been suggested by John Wheeler.

Wheeler and the Deconstruction of Natural History

John Wheeler in recent years has provided two grounds for the belief that nature is historical, if by a historical nature one means a nature the orders of which are not logocentric, or bound to eternal laws, and are generated not only by a causal mandate from the past but also by a series of partially free and contingent interpretations made in the present. First, the black hole, the big bang, and the big crunch all indicate that the laws of physics are not independent but, in a word, historically contingent. Within black holes the meaning of space, time and matter collapses, and "with that collapse the very framework falls down for anything one ever called a law of physics."[32] Wheeler adds that even "Einstein's general relativity gives not the slightest evidence whatsoever for a before before the big bang or an after after collapse. For law no other possibility is evident but that it must fade out of existence at one bound of time and come to being at the other. Law cannot stand engraved on a tablet of stone for all eternity."[33] It is apparent, then, that physical law is not independent of contingencies—that is, such law is historical. Second, quantum theory leads to the well-known uncertainty principle, that the act of observation alters the results of observation, that the manner of measurement affects the outcome of the measurement. The uncertainty principle eliminates the possibility of an absolute knowledge of the events of nature; and certainly it jeopardizes a logocentric physics, a physics that could objectively enunciate the eternal laws of nature.

It is Wheeler's extraordinary emphasis on the second point that leads to his radical interpretation of relativity and, finally, of the historicity of natural laws. If the only reality we have—because it is the only one we know—is partially dependent on observation, then, says Wheeler, reality should be treated as nothing but the interaction, the evolving relatedness, between the observer and the observed. "Reality is theory," says Wheeler, quoting Torny Segerstedt. Reality is like a special version of the game of twenty questions Wheeler once found himself unknowingly playing. When Wheeler's turn to ask the questions came, the other players secretly agreed to have no common answer. In response to each question, each player would give any answer he or she independently chose to give, subject only to one condition: it had to be consistent with what had previously been answered, even though that meant each player had continually to change his or her answer as the game progressed. After many questions, Wheeler finally guessed the "right" answer, which happened to be the word "cloud," and that was the answer then held by all players. The answers provided by the answerers (the observed) contributed their solidity to that conclusion; but also, Wheeler's choices of which questions to ask (the observer) contributed their solidity, for without Wheeler's particular questions, a different word would have resulted.

Wheeler's general conclusion is that this universe, its particularities and its laws, is "participatory" in the sense that the observer participates in reality, which always has been and always will be an observer-observed creation. Every observer's interpretive reaction contributes to present reality's new definition. A physicist's knowledge is historical not just in that it is subjectively perspectival, which even an Einstein would recognize, but in the sense that objectively, what is known—even "laws of nature"—is literally created by a historical series of observer-observed, relational events, a series that could have taken a different course at innumerable junctions.

Wheeler's participatory universe is not the creature of a solipsistic or nihilistic relativism; the universe's history is not just whatever we subjectively make it. The observed past contributes also to the interpretation, and the observer has no control over the content of that contribution. And, further, the inertia of the past is so powerful that there are scientific laws that do accurately generalize about the past and do have enormous predictive worth.

Nevertheless, the laws, instead of being eternally given, are temporally created by what precedes them, just as the "right" answer, "cloud," was temporally created by what preceded it.

And no given law is eternal, any more than "cloud" is the eternal answer to every game of twenty questions. The participatory universe has, says Wheeler, "no other than a higgledy-piggledy way to build law: out of the statistics of billions upon billions of acts of observer-participancy each of which by itself partakes of utter randomness."[34] But real law, temporary and jerry-rigged though it may be, is built.

Wheeler's historicity clearly rejects the nonhistoricity of Einstein's universe. Einstein, true to his admired Spinoza, sought that law in nature that was objective, deterministic, eternal, universal, preferably unified, and utterly independent of all observer-participancy and historical contingency. By contrast, Wheeler—to quote Freeman Dyson—would make all physical law relative to observers. He had us creating physical laws by our existence. In principle, if the role of the observers in the universe is as essential as he imagines, life may create physical laws by conscious decision. This is a radical departure from the objective reality in which Einstein believed so firmly."[35] Wheeler compared Einstein's view of the universe to his own through an illustration: for Einstein, the thing observed remains independent, safely behind a plate glass window; for Wheeler, the observer breaks the window, altering the observed thing by the act of observation, and thus altering the physical laws that describe the interaction between the observer and the thing observed.

Wheeler's participatory universe does not move beyond what Whitehead said about science and mathematics in *Modes of Thought* over forty years earlier. Whitehead contended that science has confined itself to the simplest things, which "are those widespread habits of nature that dominate the whole stretch of the universe within our remotest, vaguest observation."[36] However, he says, "None of these laws of nature gives the slightest evidence of necessity. . . . New modes of self-expression may be gaining ground. We cannot tell. But to judge by all analogy, after a sufficient span of existence our present laws will fade into unimportance."[37] Science, finally, is a simplified and generalized history of the specific, contingent, spatial, and temporal relations of nature; science is not the effort to describe some logocentric essence beyond historical change.

According to Whitehead, much the same can be side of the historicity of mathematical truths. Mathematics is misunderstood as absolute when it is called tautological, an error that emanates from Plato, who tended "to conceive of absolute reality as devoid of transition" and to think that "mathematics belonged to changeless reality."[38] It is fashionable, Whitehead said, to say "that 'twice-three' says the same thing as 'six'; so that no new truth is arrived at in the sentence. My contention is that the sentence considers a process and its issue."[39] Mathematics begins as a historical description and its laws are historically specific laws; as the structure of relations in natural process changes, the math changes also. The spatial laws of geometry, for example, are valid only for our spatiophysical epoch.[40]

Whitehead traces the scientific claim to nonhistoricity to "the disastrous separation of body and mind which has been fixed on European thought by Descartes."[41] Science fixed on the abstract generalizations of the mind, treating them as alone real and permanent. Whitehead roots the mathematical claim to nonhistoricity in Plato's mind/body dualism, which saw physical process as mere appearance and mentality as static, as alone real, and as the source of mathematics.[42]

Obviously, Whitehead would not be able to accept the limitation of Derrida's deconstructionism to the world of human expression alone. Nonhuman nature, as well as human expression, is an evolving and social consensus. Nature is historical and contingent and emerges into new spatiotemporal, or cosmic, epochs and thereby creates new interpretations of its past. Any effort to hand nature over to Newton's mechanistic logocentrism or Kant's synthetic a priori is mistaken. Finally, it is because nature reinterprets itself that science and math must be reinterpreted.

James and Dewey also reject that bifurcation that would make nature logocentric and nonhistorical.[43] James in particular anticipates Wheeler with an eerie exactness. In "Is Life Worth Living?" James asserts "that our own reactions on this world, small as they are in bulk, are integral parts of the whole thing, and necessarily help to determine the definition."[44] He quickly transfers this participatory notion to religion: "I confess that I do not see why the very existence of an invisible world may not in part depend on the personal response which any one of us may make to the religious appeal." Equally, Dewey affirms that our religious imagination can create new environments which can accomplish what otherwise cannot be accomplished.[45] For all three American philosophers, all actuality is experiential, all objects are composed of somewhat free reinterpretations of their past. Consequently, all three would accept Wheeler's participatory universe and apply his deconstructionist historical method to the affairs of nature, as well as to the world of human expression.

Wieman, Meland, and Loomer (in his later articles and papers) are equally uncompromising in their rejection of any mind/body dualism and in their insistence on the historicity of natural affairs as well as human affairs. They break with the side of Whitehead we have not discussed here—the side most evident in *Process and Reality* that allows Whitehead to find, beneath the changing laws of physical nature and mathematics that evolve through "cosmic epochs," a "metaphysical stability" yielded by the primordial nature of God.[46] For the empirical process theologians, there is nothing beyond historical interaction which, if it does exist, can be known. All that is known is historical and subject to historical examination. And from this historicist foundation, a notion of the development of historical orders in general, and of the development of the religious order and meaning of history in particular, is to be derived.

The Reconstruction of Religious History

A deconstructionist historical method would analyze the reality of the past by following the chain of signs, the writings on writings, the interpretations of interpretations, that constitute the reality of the past. It would emphasize the free augmentation of historical orders and meanings as they are constructed by ever-expanding interpretations.

That method would be incompatible with a supernaturalistic theology or with a theology whose God speaks from beyond history or with a theology that is ontological in the sense that it affirms an eternal nature of God guiding or even luring the processes of history. Derrida is remarkably specific on this point, rooting the logocentric error of the West in the theological belief that all religious signs signify something that is in some respect a pure signified, where a pure signified is a reality that depends for its significance on nothing beyond itself and thereby is ontologically independent. This is Derrida's grammatological way of rooting logocentrism in what theologians call the aseity of God. Using the word "sign" in this instance logocentrically, Derrida says: "The sign and divinity have the same place and time of birth. The age of the sign is essentially theological."[47] That age extends from Plato's *Phaedrus*, through the Christian Middle Ages, to contemporary phenomenology and structuralism; it exists wherever there is "a sign signifying a signifier itself signifying an eternal verity, eternally thought and spoken in the proximity of a present logos."[48] That age includes, I believe, the writings of Charles Hartshorne, as he attempts to describe through a priori reasoning the abstract nature of God, just as surely as it includes the writings of Karl Barth on the eternal God revealed through Jesus Christ in the witness of the Scripture and the writings of Paul Tillich on the form Being-itself.

A deconstructionist historical method accords well with the naturalism of American religious empiricism, and yet contributes to it possibilities for a more specific historicism. For a deconstructionist historical method, as well as for American religious empiricism, God is a term referring in some special way to natural and social history. God means for these movements, just as God meant for the more historicist outlooks within Hebrew and Christian religion, that general complexion or activity within history which makes history meaningful or worth living in. The deconstructionist and the American religious empiricist both recognize that God is continually reinterpreted in history. However, a deconstructionist historical method specifies the centrality of the historical meaning of theological terms, and the ways in which that historical meaning is comprised of a chain of reinterpretations.

For American religious empiricism, religion is seen to be an interpretation of the God of history. But when deconstructionism, with its specific terminology, would see religion as a writing about God, the chain of signifiers about the signified which is God, it would suggest a powerful imagery for seeing the historicity of God. The study of religion can be seen as the study, not of extra-historical realities, and not only of the social context of the Bible and the religious institutions, but of the religious community's interpretations of its God, of what it regards as the holy character of its history. Further, religion's own interpretations of God could be understood to in part alter the meaning of God, for the signifier is always capable, to some extent, of altering the meaning of the signified. Further still, the deconstructionist approach suggests ways of seeing how God acts through religion.

The deconstructionist historical method makes explicit the empiricist notion that God as the object of religious interpretations is historically effective. God the signified is real as a cause is real through its effects, as a historical event is real in the present, as any text is real to its readers. Derrida's approach could be called pragmatic[49] and would suggest a pragmatic knowledge of God similar to the pragmatic knowledge of God called for by Charles Sanders Peirce and William James. For such a pragmatic approach, God the signified would be known as one knows the evolving character of, say, a friend—through inferring the character by interpreting the effects of that friend on oneself. The pragmatic knowledge of God is illustrated in the Hebrew prophet's knowledge of God through what appear to be the effects of God in historical events. This expression of the activity of God is illuminated by the deconstructionist analysis of the effectiveness of the chain of signifiers or the effectiveness of the inertia of nature. They effectively construct and limit those interpreters who live in their historical shadow.

Further, the deconstructionist historical method makes explicit the empiricist notion that God, even as the object of religious interpretation, is not absolute. God is not purely active, but is altered by historical interpretations. God, like any signified, is affected by the signifier who interprets the signified. God, like a law of nature, is affected by the events of nature which react to the heritage of their own pasts. God, then, evolves through the workings of the interpretive historical practice. God is a chain of signifieds changing as each new signifier alters its past and then becomes part of what will be the past for future signifiers.

In fact, when the present signifier acts to alter the signified meaning of history, one could speak of God active in history—active here not as a past signified, but in the present through the act of a signifier. In this sense it makes sense to talk of God active in the religious life of the religious community, in the words of the prophet, or in the life of Jesus. Here God is active not as the heritage of past historical worth, but creatively, as the generation of new historical worth.

The question remains, Is God then merely a sign, or worse, a sign interpreted by later signs or a sign reinterpreting earlier signs? Is this not to reduce God to the status of merely grammatological device?

Derrida, as well as Wheeler, however, would never say "merely a sign." For a sign, an interpretation, is not a diminutive term; it refers, rather, to the only constituents of life. Through time, the evolution of God is the evolution of the chain of signs, or interpretations, about the worth of the historical process. This chain of signs is as much physical as it is linguistic; always it is eventful. In the moment when God functions as a past signified, pragmatically impinging on the religious individual or the religious situation, God is real as an influence is real, transforming that individual's life or the shape of the situation. In the moment when God functions as a signifier, God is real as an interpretation of the present individual. In either case, it makes sense to say God acts in history.

This deconstructionist theological historicism, first, is thoroughly consistent with American religious empiricism and second, emphasizes how, for that empiricism, the most basic reality is historical. This historicism provides a way of showing how God lives entirely within the historical chain of signs, devoid of any nonhistorical, necessary structure. And this picture bears strong resemblance to the doctrine of God held by most members of the Chicago School of theology—such as the "Creative Good" described by Wieman, the "Creative Passage" described by Meland, or "the organic restlessness of the whole body of creation" described by Loomer.

These American religious empiricists contribute to theological historicism a naturalistic component neglected, as I have noted, by Derrida's Continental humanism. Their historicism is based on empirical grounds alone, and it derives in part from what these theologians have learned from the natural sciences. Certainly these theologians relate this historicism to its biblical and doctrinal roots and construe its religious implications. If for these theologians there is a best description of the worth itself of the historical process, it is found in the tropism of all—human and nonhuman—living systems toward greater complexity. The web of relations between creatures grows increasingly complicated; human culture on the average creates individuals capable of sustaining, without disintegration, ever greater diversities of experience.

"God" is the word that points to this general and, so far, unchanging orientation of historical change. This orientation is a biological and cultural fact, typically neglected by physicists with their understandable emphasis on entropy and by theologians with their understandable emphasis on the destructiveness of human sin. But it is a fact taken with new seriousness by physicists who have read Ilya Prigogine[50] and by theologians who oppose the European neglect of the doctrine of creation.[51] It is a trend built out of "billions upon billions of acts of observer-participancy, each of which by itself partakes of utter randomness," to quote John Wheeler again. In its earthly expression, it is a trend that, given the likehood of nuclear war, may be set far back. Nevertheless, it is a trend that will have given to human history a worth that for the time being makes all the difference.

The increasing complexity of history elicits from the American religious empiricists a language about God. This complexity engenders in the beholder an aesthetic response, which can be termed a religious experience on at least two grounds: first, it appears to be caused by a character to history which seems to be nowhere completely absent; second, it is an experience that is intrinsically valuable and, possibly, life-sustaining.

According to this distinctively American, empirical, and processive interpretation, aesthetic complexity is augmented by the signifier's continual reinterpretation of the signified worth of the historical process. If God the signifier is the interpretive writing about that worth, then this is how God is creative; if religion is the interpretive writing about God, then this is how religion is creative.

Religion as the chain of reinterpretations of historical worth is not the imitation of an eternal truth. Religion is partially free, literally made in and through history; the conclusions of religion, much like Wheeler's "laws of nature," are made in and through relations through time. Religion construed in this way is not the effort to specify and worship what is universal and eternal and, "therefore," divine. (It does not seek to worship, for example, Paul Tillich's structure of Being-itself or Whitehead's primordial nature of God.) Religion, at least in the West, is not mainly about the discovery of metaphysical orders but about the development of historical orders.

Here, the religious person would be distinguished from the nonreligious person by his or her faith that the tropism toward greater historical value is real and that it can be sustained through reinterpretation. This tropism is a movement toward greater complexity. By tropism toward greater complexity I refer to what Loomer called size (diversity within a sustainable unity) or to what Whitehead called contrast.[52] Complexity has two aspects: 1) a width of data, giving both a social diversity and the throttle for growth through an acquaintance with strange options; and 2) a narrowness of concentration, giving both a depth through focus and an intensity of experience. Now faith in the reality of this historical movement, in this tropism toward complexity, is itself creative, and is the creativity specific to a religious person. In a truly Jamesian manner, this "faith in a fact can help create the fact," for faith in the tropism toward complexity can enable the religious contribution to complexity.[53] James extends this notion into a comment on God when he says,

> I confess that I do not see why the very existence of an invisible world may not in part depend on the personal response which

any one of us may make to the religious appeal. God himself, in
short, may draw vital strength and increase of very being from
our fidelity. For my own part, I do not know what the sweat and
blood and tragedy of this life means, if they mean anything short
of this. If this life be not a real fight, in which something is
eternally gained for the universe by success, it is no better than a
game of private theatricals from which one may withdraw at
will.[54]

Then, as a radical empiricist, James adds: "But it *feels* like a real
fight—as if there were something really wild in the universe
which we, with all our idealities and faithfulnesses, are needed to
redeem."[55]

   This faith cannot be translated directly into an optimism
about moral progress in history. In fact, moral optimism in the
thought of empirical religious liberals is far less prevalent than is
commonly thought.[56] To believe that the complexity of the
historical process will increase is first of all to comment directly
only on a growth of aesthetic value. That growth sometimes has
mixed moral results, providing as much potential for good as for
ill.[57] It may include, for example, the increase in the aesthetic
complexity of the techniques of warfare, which may lead to
history's effective termination.

   On the other hand, a religious faith in the tropism toward
complexity can have moral effects. That faith can become the
basis for an aesthetic ethic, the aim of which is to act so as to
enable others to participate in and to appreciate the evolutionary
movement toward greater complexity. And this, in turn, can lead
to practical steps for extending that participation and appreciation to those who are deprived of it.[58]

   Again, it might be asked, Why God? We have acknowledged
that God is literally embodied in the life of the religious individual who functions as a past or present signifier of the worth of
the historical process. If God is real only in the experiences of
religious individuals, whether human or nonhuman, why not
forget God and focus instead on the common creature's drive for
increasing complexity? Does not the abandonment of logocentrism in the thorough sense advocated by Derrida, Wheeler, and
the Chicago theologians eventually show that God-language is

tied to the faith in the eternal, so that to abandon logocentrism is to abandon religious rhetoric and religious faith?

Perennially, this question has confronted American religious empiricism. In the present context, it might be best to respond to it by affirming a sense of history, if the word "sense" is used in the radical way intended by the radical empiricists—as not only the five senses' perception of facts but also as the appreciative sense of the value in the objective relations between the facts. The sense of history so interpreted, while it is always specific in its focus, can be attended also by an appreciative awareness of history's general tropism toward greater complexity. That appreciation can be marked by a feeling for that tropism's apparent contingency—that the historical process could have been bent toward the reduction of aesthetic complexity, that there is no clear mechanical or biological reason why it was not, and that nevertheless it is bent toward increasing complexity.[59]

This apparently contingent tropism toward complexity is the empirically perceived historical condition that provides much of that vitality which makes life, including human life, possible and valuable. Exactly because it is not explicable logocentrically or through some doctrine of eternal and divine *telos* imposed on the world, it is a surd and a source of that wonder and mystery that is appropriately thought of as religious.[60] Hence, the use of the word "God" to describe the tropism.

Certainly, it is individuals who augment the chain of signs, who augment the stream of life experience by subjectively reinterpreting the worth of the historical process with ever increasing complexity. But that does not diminish the religious wonder and mystery of the historical tendency that they embody—any more than Christian acts of love diminish the divine love that is said to live in those acts.

So, the sense of history is a radically empirical sense of the aesthetic importance of a general tendency throughout history. Further, it is an appreciation of each particular instance of increasing complexity as an instance of the general movement of history, of each reinterpretation of worth as an instance of the general tropism toward greater aesthetic complexity. The religious dimension of that sense of history is the appreciation of both the utter contingency and the utter importance of that tropism; it is the wonder attending the awareness of that tropism.

This interpretation of the religious sense uses God-language to refer to the evolving orders and meanings of religious history. God, so conceived, is dynamic and as dynamic can be grounded to some extent in the Bible. Referring to the ancient Hebrew community, Robert B. Laurin has said, "The fact that the traditions were changed, modified, and expanded by the community at various periods, shows significantly that the basic stance of the people of God toward tradition was always to a dynamically involved one, since Yahweh was dynamic and developing his will."[61] Equally, the Chicago theologians point to God's dynamic contribution to the historical process. I refer to Wieman, who sensed God as "the creation of a more inclusive unity of events and possibilities";[62] to Meland, who senses God as "being of a piece with the Creative Passage" and "the Creative Passage as being the most basic characterization of existence as it applies to all life";[63] and to Loomer, who associates God with "the creative advance of the web of life."[64] Each of these thinkers refused to identify God with a logos above the world, let alone with a supernatural being beyond the world. For each of them, God is found empirically in the world process and religiously in the developing complexity of the world's historical order.

Deconstructionism, in short, suggests a working approach to history. It offers the beginnings of a historicist hermeneutic for American religious empiricism. If such an approach to history were developed, it might be possible to fulfill a dream sometimes implicit in American religious empiricism, but a dream never fulfilled by the empiricists themselves: to move beyond metaphysical abstractions and systematically to use immediate experience to interpret the particular religious meanings of living local histories.

An Explanation: Deconstruction and Historical Generalization

Finally, however, it appears incongruous to claim from a deconstructionist standpoint that there is a "general tropism" towards aesthetic complexity or that the word "God" is meaningful. Deconstructionism, after all, is a sustained protest against not only the nakedly Platonic logocentrisms of Western culture, but against any escape from the chain of texts, any escape into a region from which one could make pronouncements about what is general. Derrida negatively characterizes Western metaphysics as "a linked chain of determinations of the center," a series of new names for the metaphysical structure. He says, "The history of metaphysics, like the history of the West, is the history of these metaphors and metonymies. . . . It could be shown that all the names related to fundamentals, to principles, or to the center have always designated an invariable presence—*eidos, arche, telos, energeia, ousia* (essence, existence, substance, subject) alētheia, transcendentality, consciousness, God, man, and so forth."[65] Are then the designations, "general tropism" and even "God," only alternative metaphors suggesting alternative metaphysics of presence? If so, how can they be dropped into a deconstructionist discussion attacking such metaphors?

This apparent inconsistency diminishes when it is realized that Derrida's strictures are directed towards the metaphysics of being, whereas the generalizations of American religious empiricism are features of becoming, or history. All the terms cited by Derrida above are terms attached to the metaphysics of being, or substance. Derrida is particularly explicit in his reference to the metaphysics of being when he says "speaking" attempts to reveal the presence of being, or when he says that "phonocentrism merges with the historical determination of the meaning of being in general as *presence*."[66] Derrida is concerned to avoid the illusion and the prison-house of those Western thinkers who posit a static structure of being and thereby deny history and its rhetorical development of ideas. By contrast, the generalizations of American religious empiricism are about becoming rather than being, about history rather than substance. Consequently, the deconstructionist indictment of a metaphysics of being does not apply to American religious empiricism.

But this defense may not be sufficient. For it could be argued that any generalization, even one about becoming, even one about historical process, is suspiciously metaphysical. It is, after all, still a generalization, and for deconstructionist historicism, which intends to stay close to the particularities of history, it well could be termed unacceptable.

However, this is an argument which could not be consistently sustained by the deconstructionist. For deconstructionism itself generalizes, and thus must tolerate, the limited generalizations about history issued by others. M. H. Abrams and Wayne Booth in a 1977 issue of *Critical Inquiry* quite effectively make this case.

Abrams notes that Derrida's "graphocentric premises eventuate in what is patently a metaphysics, a world-view of the free and unceasing play of *differance* which . . . we are not able to name."[67] Derrida repeatedly makes the metaphysical claim, "*Il n'y a pas d'hors-texte,*" (there is nothing outside the text). If the deconstructionist critique of generalization is taken literally, says Abrams in a later publication, then deconstructionism "cannot in fact escape the orbit of the linguistic system it deconstructs," "the deconstructive instruments deconstruct themselves." Abrams backs this charge with an admission from Derrida himself: "the enterprise of deconstruction always in a certain way falls prey to its own work."[68] But Derrida does keep writing, and in that most important sense his deconstructionism is not deconstructed. Apparently, deconstructionists do permit themselves certain minimal generalizations; accordingly, they cannot fault American religious empiricists simply on the grounds that they generalize.

Wayne Booth makes the same point when he asks the deconstructionists for justice in literary criticism, for the deconstructionists to tolerate in others the sort of generalities (Booth says "monisms") they use themselves.[69] Every deconstructionist seeks understanding every time he or she speaks or writes. Every deconstructionist, in this act, assumes that there are limits to pluralism, that we are not entirely isolated in our separate worlds, and assumes a kind of practical monism. Further, the deconstructionist is a monist also in attempting to develop a better literary-critical theory, and in expecting a just treatment in that undertaking. This too presumes that there are limits to pluralism, that there is a common world of literature, and that it makes sense to ask about better and worse theories about that world. Booth's argument is that the deconstructionists cannot in justice reject out of hand the monisms of alternative literary critical theories when they themselves are covert monists. Clearly, the same would apply in theology: the deconstructionists should not reject out of hand the generalizations implicit in American religious empriricism.

Of course, this in no way assures the truth of American religious empiricism's generalizations. The best evidence for these generalizations may lie in natural history, particularly the movement through that curve of complexity described by biological evolution. But the history of human communities shows, equally, a tendency toward greater aesthetic complexity, seen most clearly when the earliest periods of recorded history, despite their unexpected sophistication, are compared to the latest periods. Nevertheless, generalizations of this scope have not been carefully validated by empirical theologians—nor, perhaps, can they be. In fact, American religious empiricists are so lacking in that metaphysical confidence found in those who have extra-historical foundations that they seldom argue systematically for the truth of their empirical generalizations. Further, and to push beyond the bounds of this discussion, American religious empiricists are so lacking in the confidence so typical of Western philosophy that they tend to possess "a tragic sense of life," to use Sydney Hook's expression.

Chapter 3

A Pragmatic Interpretation: The Tragedy of the Liberals

That life is *not* worth living the whole army of suicides declare,—an army whose roll-call, like the famous evening gun of the British army, follows the sun round the world and never terminates. We, too, as we sit here in our comfort, must "ponder these things" also, for we are of one substance with these suicides, and their life is the life we share.[1]

W illiam James then went on to weigh the haunting implications of that statement in his essay, "Is Life Worth Living?" The same William James is a central figure in American liberal religious thought, a movement commonly dismissed as naively optimistic. Sydney Ahlstrom speaks for that consensus when he concludes his discussion of liberal theology in *A Religious History of the American People* with the famous passage from H. Richard Niebuhr, which claims that in liberalism "a God without wrath brought men without sin into a kingdom without judgment through the ministrations of a Christ without a cross."[2]

The outlook of the liberals and of James was misunderstood partly because they, in James's terms, went on to ask, "What reasons can we plead that may render such a brother (or sister) willing to take up the burden again?"[3] To the critics of liberalism this hope for a therapeutic answer may have been enough to invite the opprobrious designation, "optimistic."

However, Shailer Mathews, an empirical liberal of the Chicago School of theology, protested in 1936, "We pioneers were optimistic enough to believe it was possible to develop a social conscience, but did not suffer from the illusions with which we have been charged."[4] Certain critics of liberalism, Mathews said, attribute to liberalism "a blind faith in progress and a minimizing of sin." "I once tried," he added, "to get from one of our critics the names of those he had in mind, but could get only general statements."[5]

Reinhold Niebuhr was not unwilling to name names. In his 1935 *An Interpretation of Christian Ethics* he volunteered that Shailer Mathews made statements which were "strikingly naive," and that Mathews's colleague Gerald Birney Smith collaborated in liberalism's "monotonous reiteration of the pious hope that people might be good and loving."[6] In his subsequent Gifford Lectures he informed his audience that "The modern naturalist, whether romantic or rationalistic, has an easy conscience because he believes that he has not strayed very far from, and can easily return to, the innocency of nature."[7]

Mathews, while wounded by statements like those from Niebuhr, seems never to have noted that it was Niebuhr and his neo-orthodox colleagues who insisted on limiting the effects of evil. They, in Niebuhr's words, concluded that the Christian has a home only outside of history, and that in history the Christian rightly felt an "essential homelessness."[8] It was Niebuhr who restricted evil by protecting an unambiguously good God from contamination in historical evil. Nor did Mathews contrast Niebuhr's equivocating realism (which confined evil to what is of secondary importance) to his own unappreciated gravity, which found evil in his own home and in the only arena of his God— that is, in history.

However much Mathews may have overlooked in his critics, his protestations had their validity, at least for those more empirical liberals whose roots can be traced to the British empirical Enlightenment. Mathews's protestations spoke not only for himself, but for such Chicago School empirical liberals as Shirley Jackson Case, Bernard Meland, and Bernard Loomer. In fact, it appears that their temperament deep within was more tragic than optimistic.

Mathews's protestations may not always apply to the more pietistic and romantic liberals, those who floated in the ocean stream which left Germany as an epistemological idealism (of Kant, Schleiermacher, Hegel, Schelling, Fichte, etc.), washed over England (especially, Coleridge), and arrived in America originally as Transcendentalism, and later as particular phases of nineteenth and twentieth century liberal religious thought. These pietistic liberals, from Emerson and Bushnell through Paul Tillich, were sometimes historical optimists, sometimes not. The important point is that for them some transcendental absolute shining through history, and not historical experience itself, is the source of what is real.

Unlike the pietistic liberals, the empirical liberals could not find the holy through transcendental, rationalist, or romantic vision. Unlike the neo-orthodox and the fundamentalist thinkers who came to surround them, the empirical liberals could not look to a redemptive process which intervened in the natural course of events. This all meant that the empirical liberals had to live without the luxury of clarity, a clarity which enabled the neo-orthodox and the fundamentalist to prosecute those who lacked clarity—about the wrath of God, the sin of humanity, the judgment of the kingdom, the cross of Christ. The empirical liberals did not have a God who came from beyond history to rescue (through an idealistic vision or a supernatural victory) humanity from its confinement in history. Instead, the empirical liberals were caught in an endlessly complex social and natural history, aided only by a God within history who left humanity within history to live with the consequences of its own historical successes and failures. Add to this that today, as we live knowingly in an entropic nature and in a social history dominated by the spectre of nuclear war, the liberal commitment to history seems to be a commitment to something doomed. It is all the more ironic, then, that those who still hold for a God-led escape from history should continue to call the empirical liberals optimistic.

For the empirical liberal pragmatism was the principle effort to fight the tragedy implicit in this confinement to history. While this is never stated in so many words by the empirical liberals, it is implicit in their labors. William James's own career demonstrates it over and over. His depressive inaction around 1870 was answered by his practical decision to believe in his capacity to act freely. His basically phenomenological work as a psychologist from 1870 to 1900 was answered by his basically pragmatic work as a philosopher from 1900 to 1910. His poignant recognition of the "army of suicides" who declare "that life is *not* worth living," led him pragmatically to ask, "What reasons can we plead that may render such a brother (or sister) willing to take up the burden again?" Pragmatism used history to respond to the tragedy of history. The same historicism which had removed the extra-historical security still embraced by the critics of the liberals could be used by pragmatism to find a working response—one better than sheer passivity to historical fatedness.

But this pragmatism was not merely formal, trusting in the sheer procedure of testing ideas by examining their historical consequences. Pragmatism for James needed a content, a content provided by the religious experience made still-meaningful by his radical empiricism. For James as a radical empiricist was an empiricist who moved beyond the British empiricists, to accept what he saw as the fact that we experience historical values with our whole selves just as surely as we experience colors with our eyes. Hence, he could hope to experience "reasons" to take up the burden again. So James argued for some sort of "over-belief," some answer that committed him to one side in the contests of the world. Life, James said, "*feels* like a real fight," and we have no choice but to take a stand and to fight.[9] The liberal theologians agreed, and fought, in turn, for their Christian overbeliefs. Consequently, the history used by the liberals to respond to history's tragedy was a value-laden history.

But, finally, it was the empiricism which caused the trouble. For this unblinking regard for what is sensed, without recourse to what is not sensed, meant one had to cast his or her lot with the contingencies of history. If history was a perilous struggle, and this seemed to be what Darwin was telling the pragmatists and the liberals, well then, God itself and the values promoted by God were caught in that perilous struggle, for they existed within history, or they did not exist at all. Hence, the tragic outlook. History would contain all the values and all the Gods there ever would be. If history, itself, taught no happy resolution, there was nowhere else to get one. The cold empirical look at history required by such an empiricism allowed no recourse to a rationally demonstrated God (as in Locke's An Essay Concerning Human Understanding, or to a God known by extra-historical emotion or vision (the pietistic liberals) or to a God known through the extra-historical Word (the neo-orthodox successors to liberalism) or to a God found in the extra-historical miracle (the fundamentalists). The radical empiricist and his or her values and God were caught within a time-bound, Darwinian history.

For James in particular, to live within history is "really dangerous."[10] It is to reject what James called "the prodigal son attitude" toward life. "I am willing," said James, "that there should be real losses and real losers, and no total preservation of all that is."[11] Losses are inevitable and they cost. There is no opportunity to say, In the eyes of history I may have failed, but in the eyes of the Eternal (Lord, Reason, Purpose, whatever) I am a success and will be remembered forever. The empirical liberal knows that it is possible to misread the religious meaning of history. This makes the careful use of pragmatism all the more important. But there is always the chance that pragmatism will pursue the wrong value. Hence, even pragmatism cannot overcome the tragic uncertainty implicit in the historicism of the empirical liberal. It is this paradox of pragmatism's strength and impotency which the critics of religious liberalism missed when they dismissed the liberals as optimistic.

My task, however, is not to describe the turns on this American route to the tragic, a story told in one way already by Sydney Hook in his essay, "Pragmatism and the Tragic Sense of Life."[12] It is to discuss how pragmatism was used as a tactic for moving beyond this tragic situation. But since even pragmatism, while helpful, remained unsuccessful as a device for overcoming tragedy, my real task will be to describe how an effort to avoid the tragic in fact extended the tragic.

Weak Pragmatism and Historical Obscurity

The empirical liberals confronted two utterly serious problems, neither of which were felt by those same religious critics who said the liberals were optimistic. First, the empirical liberals' willing suspension of belief in an idealistic, supernaturalistic, or dogmatic source of religious knowledge, their willing confinement of religious knowledge to what could be gained empirically, meant that religious knowledge was, at best, obscure. What I will call "weak pragmatism" was an effort to address the problem of the obscurity of religious knowledge. Second, the empirical liberals' acceptance of evolutionary thought meant that religious knowledge, like all other living realities, was emergent. Consequently, to diminish the obscurity, or to know better, what an earlier people believed is not directly to diminish the confusion of the present generation as it seeks its own appropriate belief. What I will call "strong pragmatism" was an effort to address the problem of the emergence of religious knowledge, as it affects the current generation.

A variation on weak pragmatism was utilized by Shirley Jackson Case, a New Testament scholar and church historian at The University of Chicago from 1908 to 1938. Case affirmed that the task of the biblical scholar or of the church historian was not to record the scriptural or the dogmatic evidence, but to discover the beliefs which generated the scripture or the dogma— for the scripture and dogma were the children of the parenting beliefs, and, contrary to prevailing opinion, it was not the other way around. But Case's empiricism, his desire to know the concrete and living belief, as opposed to the literary record, set for him a difficult task. How was he to discover that actual belief of a people, if that could not be identified with the literary document? There was a possible solution, in that a belief might be detected by the perceptions it caused. A belief heightens a people's "capacity for peering behind the veil of material existence to catch fresh glimpses of spiritual reality."[13] But while this religious perception might enable the scholar to reason backwards, from the perception to the probable belief which had made it possible, how is it possible to discover the religious perception itself? Recognizing this difficulty, Case's solution was to look at the social life of a people, something the empiricist could get evidence for, and to reason backwards from that social life to the probable belief which had caused it. Case's motto was that a belief's "functional efficiency is the measure of its worth."[14] In effect, Case said: look at the socio-historical practice, treat this as a function of a belief, and infer the belief from its probable functional result.

Case's solution was pragmatic, in that it discovered a meaning or a truth by looking at a consequence. Behind his solution was the current of thought established by the pragmatisms of William James and John Dewey, and pervasive of the atmosphere at The University of Chicago in the persons of George Herbert Mead, Edward Scribner Ames, and numerous others.[15] Like Case, James and Dewey had recognized religious perception as a viable form of empirical experience. As a radical empiricist, James spoke of the capacity to experience the relations between entities, bodily sensing the tensions and harmonies implicit in those relations, and experiencing therein the roots of what might be called aesthetic, moral, and religious perception.[16] Dewey, in turn, spoke of sensing, for example, the mysterious wholeness suggested by a work of art.[17]

James and Dewey, like Case, recognized, further, that beliefs could enhance such religious perceptivity. Their own philosophical writings were pragmatically justified as attempts to foster beliefs which, in turn, would open people to perceptions of value.

However, like Case again, James and Dewey had no opportunity to discover whether a belief was true by examining the kind of religious perception it caused, for such perceptions could not be examined. It is true that values are perceived or experienced, but it is also true that we cannot isolate and examine a religious perception, and consequently cannot reason from perception to an exploration of the belief which may be associated with it. Perceptions of value are often so obscure as to be unconscious, and at best they are no clearer than experience at the edge of sleep. James's and Dewey's radical empiricism, their confinement of value experience to the forms of empirical perception, had cursed them with a terrible obscurity. If these perceptions are a "buzzing blooming confusion," how is one to reason backwards from them to discover the beliefs they confirm?

James and Dewey enlarged their approach, and answered this obscurity by proposing a pragmatism which looked not to the empirically obscure perceptions resulting from a belief, but to the obvious social behaviors resulting from a belief. Their advice to the historian would be to examine the social practices of a people, and reason from them back to the beliefs which could have caused them. There, in that practice, is found the less obscure and thereby the more authoritative evidence for whether a belief was authentic for a historic people. Here pragmatism could attack the obscurity of history by turning from religious perception to social practice.

This is a "weak pragmatism" because it asks how a belief might integrate with a known history, rather than change that history. This pragmatism certainly did not eliminate the obscurity of history, for there was never any certainty about what a social practice was or what belief might have prompted it. But it did diminish the obscurity predominant in an unaided, radically empirical view of history.

Strong Pragmatism and Historical Emergence

Here the plot thickens. The weak pragmatic method might appear to clarify history's meaning for a present people when it clarifies history's meaning for a past people. It might pragmatically be established that the early church held a particular belief about an event in its history; then it might seem that a later people should accept for itself that same belief about that event. It might be naturally assumed that the meaning of history is what it is, and is unaffected by the passage of time. As the hymn says about the old time religion, if it's good enough for Paul and Silas, it's good enough for me.

Case accepted, however, the full implications of evolution. He was not prepared to acknowledge that there was a continuity through history which would permit us to generalize from the past to the present. Not only are literatures, rational ideas, or positivistic sense impressions to be de-authorized; so is past history. A belief which might once have produced beneficial religious perceptions, and therefore be true then, might not be true for a person in the twentieth century. According to Case, when we evaluate the present worth of past beliefs, our only authority is present experience as it tests the present uses of those beliefs. Certainly, weak pragmatism may reduce the obscurity of the past sufficiently for us to conclude what was believed by an earlier people. But in our efforts to determine what is presently true for us, those past truths are, says Case, never more than didactic or stimulative.[18]

Perhaps, suggested Case, there were in the lives of biblical peoples supernatural meanings to history, where ostensible miracles promoted religious perceptions, and thereby were true for them. Perhaps such a supernaturalistic ascription is today not only avoidable, but is damaging, and thereby is not true.[19] In short, historical meanings are not only obscure, but also emergent, so that what might be true, or beneficial, for one generation may be untrue to a succeeding generation. This is what the emergence of history requires, where the emergence of history refers to the unpredictable novelties of historical development.

If radical empiricism undercuts the clarity of the past, emergentism undercuts the hoped-for continuities of history, making, for example, the notion of "the holy catholic church" a comment not on an enduring communal essence, but on a chain of events, sometimes consistent through time, sometimes inconsistent.

Emergence is driven by "variation," as that notion is described in Darwin's The Origin of the Species. Variation is the unpredictable introduction of novel possibilities into the pool of what is inherited; it eliminates any mechanistic continuity in biological life.

Emergence was philosophically generalized beyond biology by a number of late nineteenth and early twentieth century thinkers, among them William James. In 1880 James lectured on "Great Men and Their Environment," arguing against the selectivist interpretation of social evolution then being advanced by Herbert Spencer and his disciples. Spencer had so emphasized the importance of environment in determining the present course of events that nothing was left to the initiatives and decisions of individuals. Now it is true, James acknowledged, that Darwin spent most of his time showing how environments do the selecting. But that in no way diminishes the importance of "spontaneous variation," which Darwin fully accepted. When Spencer so exclusively emphasized environment, he depreciated the spontaneous arrival of the pecularities which the environment selects. James's prime illustration is the great man, who is related to the selectivity of the environment in exactly the way that the variation is related to the environment in Darwinian evolution. "The causes of production of great men lie," said James, "in a sphere wholly inaccessible to the social philosopher. He must simply accept geniuses as data, just as Darwin accepts his spontaneous variation."[20] The great individuals are "the mutations of societies."[21]

Here James is laying the foundations for a notion of emergence in social history. The point is that social mutations create new truths, so that what was not at one time true can become true. As James said, "Truths emerge from facts; but they dip forward into facts again and add to them; which facts again create or reveal new truth . . . and so on indefinitely."[22]

Historical emergence rendered old truths inadequate and led James to introduce a form of pragmatism as the best way of selecting new truths. The pragmatic response to the obscurity of history asks whether a historical meaning or belief fits into a given historical selection. The pragmatic response to the emergence of history asks whether a new historical meaning might function as a beneficial historical variation in a current historical situation. This latter pragmatic response might need even to imagine future social mutations and to ask whether a new belief might some day work beneficially or harmfully in possible histories yet to come. I will call this second pragmatism "strong pragmatism" because it uses pragmatism to create new beliefs and new truths, and thereby change present history, rather than to understand how an idea has integrated with a past history.

Following this Jamesean approach, Shirley Jackson Case made present experience alone authoritative as the pragmatic testing ground for present religious beliefs. New variations on beliefs were to be evaluated in terms of their capacity to engender beneficial social consequences in the present generation. Old beliefs, if they failed to engender beneficial social consequences in the present generation, were to be considered no longer true for the present generation.

However, even as Case applied it, this strong pragmatism did no more than alleviate the confusion introduced by historical emergence, for there could be no real confidence that what appeared to be the belief most capable of generating beneficial social circumstances was that belief in fact. Conceivably, and as often happens, a belief thought to be beneficial turns out to be harmful to a society. (For example, at least certain aspects of social welfare programs seem to be suffering that fate in late twentieth century America; or, pure socialist economies may be suffering that fate in nations like China.) The result is often a persisting confusion about what is most beneficial and most true in the way of religious beliefs. Compared to the certainty of those who criticized the empirical liberals, this uncertainty can assume tragic proportions.

Valuational Pragmatism and the Capacity to Take a Stand

Strong pragmatism is further weakened, then, because it does not indicate which novel future is truly beneficial in a particular historical situation. Strong pragmatism can be used just as well to support the Third Reich as to support the Third World. The values appropriate for historical action are not discovered by strong pragmatism—nor by weak pragmatism, for that matter. Even with these tools of pragmatism there remains a tragic uncertainty about what counts as a beneficial religious perception or a beneficial way of life.

William James may have appeared to answer this uncertainty by introducing a subjectivistic and aesthetic criterion. He said that we eventually accept religious beliefs because "we take an immediate delight in them; or else it is because we believe them to bring us good consequential fruits for life."[23] The good consequential fruits are in James's account seen to be good because they, like the immediate reaction, are delight-producing. According to James, religion in its twice born sense is the opposite of acedia, anhedonia, or a bottomless kind of despair.[24] Religious conduct of all sorts should lead to feelings which "Kant calls 'sthenic' affection, an excitement of the cheerful, expansive, 'dynamogenic' order which, like any tonic, freshens our vital powers."[25] Religious conclusions are beneficial, in short, when they instill, sooner or later, experiences which are satisfying. If a religious position is seen to deal with "1. An uneasiness; and 2. Its solution,"[26] it is declared to be true.

This aestheticism cannot be dismissed as mere hedonism. For, James would argue, a merely immediate and hedonistic delight must be balanced against the remote delights or pains ensuing from the pursuit of the immediate delight. Any belief, to be deemed beneficial, must "bear the criticisms of the convalescent hour" and fit consistently with "our other opinions" or "our needs." James goes on to say, "What immediately feels most 'good' is not always most 'true,' when measured by the verdict of the rest of experience. The difference between Philip drunk and Philip sober is the classic instance in corroboration."[27] Or, "the greatest enemy of any one of our truths may be the rest of our truths."[28]

Even if this aestheticism is not hedonistic, it is, however, subjectivistic in that "delight," "cheerful," or "feels good" is a judgment confined to one's own subjective sensibilities. This subjectivism has earned the current approval of Richard Rorty. In one of the essays of Consequences of Pragmatism, Rorty praises James's subjectivism. James and Nietzsche, Rorty says, "were the first generation not to believe that they had the truth. So they were content to have no answer to the question, 'Where do you stand when you say all these terrible things about other people?' They were content to take the halo off words like 'truth,' 'science' and 'knowledge' and 'reality,' rather than to offer a view about the nature of the things named by these words."[29] Rorty suggests that all that is left is aesthetic activity,[30] a genteel conversation among people holding incommensurable notions.[31] Now Rorty is a pragmatist in that he believes that the conservation should be "edifying," that it should be useful, and that it should be socially beneficial in that it takes us most directly, without intermediate metaphysical constructs, to our relations with people.[32] However, Rorty is ruthlessly unequivocal in claiming that pragmatism settles no disputes about what is objectively valuable, provides no place to stand in the major dilemmas and disputes of history.

Rorty acknowledges that to our pre-pragmatistic sensibilities the possibility that all criteria are "no more than temporary resting places, constructed by a community to facilitate its inquiries, seems morally humiliating."[33] There is then no way to condemn the secret police, there is no way to object to the fascist, at least if by "a way" one means a way of saying that there is something absolute beyond ourselves which would condemn a practice. For, as Rorty says, "there is nothing deep down inside us except what we have put there ourselves."[34] Rorty's pragmatic method then ends in subjectivism, no matter how much Rorty the man wants philosophy to address human relations. Certainly, Rorty's subjectivism is not a subjectivism of the idealist or of the existentialist sort; but it is the subjectivism of a method without access to anything outside the self.

It is just such subjectivism which a few younger neopragmatists are currently protesting. Cornel West has argued that Richard Rorty has stopped short of recognizing the truly objective function of philosophy, most particularly, that philosophy has a political function. Rorty had concluded, that after the false idealisms, scientisms, and existentialisms have been expunged from philosophy, that after all philosophical claims to suprahistorical reference have been rejected, that then we will be left with nothing more to do than to converse, knowing that there is nothing between us to make our various positions commensurable.[35] West objects not to Rorty's antirealism, antifoundationalism, nor to his detranscendentalization of the subject, nor to Rorty's reversion to pragmatism, but to Rorty's willingness arbitrarily and subjectivistically to limit philosophy to the intellectual conversation so congenial to the university intellectual. West objects on grounds that Rorty has already pointed out, and on which Rorty's pragmatist predecessors have stood—that is, on the grounds of history. Rorty has historicized philosophy, claiming to deconstruct it, to show that it is a kind of writing (in the Derridean sense), that it is a chain of interpretations, that it is "words all the way down." But, arbitrarily and inexplicably, Rorty has stopped short with intellectual history. Rorty's historicism is, in West's words, "thin": "To deconstruct the privileged notions of objectivity, universality and transcendentality without acknowledging and accenting the oppressive deeds done under the aegis of these notions is to write a thin (i.e., intellectual and homogeneous) history; that is, a history which fervently attacks epistemological privilege but remains relatively silent about political, economic, racial and sexual privilege."[36] Consistency requires, West argues, a thick historicism: "Yet after the philosophical smoke clears, the crucial task is to pursue thick (i.e., social and heterogeneous) historical accounts for the emergence, development, sustenance and decline of particular vocabularies in the natural and human sciences against the backdrop of dynamic changes in specific (and often coexisting) modes of production, political conflicts, cultural configurations and personal turmoil."[37] Instead, according to West, Rorty tends to ignore social history and to justify conclusions on nothing more significant than a subjective preference which authorizes the genteel lifestyle of the university intellectual. West is equally critical of what he considers the narrowness of Willard Quine, Roy Sellars, Nelson Goodman, and Thomas Kuhn. These ahistorical judgments leave us "hanging in a limbo."[38]

West's arguments are antisubjectivist and pro-objectivist in the sense that they woo the philosopher away from a preferential and arbitrary limitation to merely congnitive interaction, and towards a recognition of philosophy's social, political, and economic sources and effects. West has subsequently delivered on his own mandate: his Prophesy Deliverance! An Afro-American Revolutionary Christianity sets racism, Christian identity, and the Afro-American Christian response to racism in a full and "thick history" of social, political, economic, and cultural thought, instead of adopting the typically tight focus on theology and race alone.[39] West's point is reinforced by Mark Lilla, who criticizes Goodman, Hilary Putnam, and Rorty because, in properly denying the givenness of ideas or facts, they have forgotten the true givenness of the social tradition out of which they work.[40]

Frank Lentricchia has taken a similar stance against Paul de Man's deconstructionism. In his *Criticism and Social Change* Lentricchia claims that de Man's deconstructionist criticism, ironically, is ultimately formalistic; as such, it neglects the social and political functions of writing. Lentricchia takes his stand with Kenneth Burke, who argued that the writer has social obligations. Burke functions as Lentricchia's American empiricist, his way into the thick history to which any intellectual must be attentive (just as William Carlos Williams functioned, in turn, as Burke's American poet of thick history.)[41] In *Criticism and Social Change* and in his *After the New Criticism*, Lentricchia's larger point is that all formalisms in literary criticism are ultimately self-indulgent, subjective preferences, and should be replaced with a historicist objectivism which recognizes the social and political obligations of the writer.[42]

For Lentricchia, as well as for West, the irony doubles: not only does the deconstructionism of certain critics become a thinly historical formalism; the thin history, on closer inspection, appears to be a thick history. Regarded pragmatically, the thin historicist is really taking one side in what James called a forced option. By doing nothing about the political issues of the day, the thin historicism loses its innocence. It functionally collaborates with the surrounding and prevailing capitalist, bourgeois policies, just as for James the agnostic functionally collaborates with the atheist.

West, Lilla, and Lentricchia are playing out a theme implicit in James, for—contrary to Rorty's account—James was not content to leave the matter with an aestheticism of subjective taste. Far from saying, in Rorty's image, that he had to answer to the question "where do you stand when you say all these terrible things about other people?" James argued that we have a "right" to supplement our subjective beliefs with a trust in the external world, which at that point he described as "an unseen spiritual order," and then to test that trust pragmatically.[43] This amounts to a move from an apparent thin historicism to a thick historicism, although James emphasizes the historicism of psychological thickness while West and Lentricchia emphasize the historicism of political thickness.

For James, then, a trust in the spiritual order, a trust James would later call an overbelief, enabled him to move beyond the tragedy of subjectivism to a kind of objectivism. Admittedly, Rorty's claim that James has no place to stand is correct to the extent that James affirms that our values are authorized by no transcendental reality or mechanistic order. But James, rather than commit the fallacy of the excluded middle, refused to move from the denial of transcendentalism or mechanism simply to subjectivism. He embraced an objective truth of another sort— something local, transient, but valuable nevertheless. In this way James stood with statements which were true not only to the experiencer, but also to the world experienced. Hence, a merely subjectivistic aestheticism remained even for James a tragic non-answer, a consignment to impotent aporia, useless indecision. Equally, West's Afro-American revolutionary Christianity and Lentricchia's Gramscian Marxism represent such third option objectivisms, analogous to James's "overbelief" in an objective order which may not be eternal, may not be universal, but is nevertheless real. When they chose a third option, they made a move Richard Bernstein memorialized in the title of his 1983 book, *Beyond Objectivism and Relativism.*[44] They made a move Jeffrey Stout called "the new historicism" in his 1981 *The Flight from Authority: Religion, Morality and the Quest for Autonomy.* Stout's book is the most complete discussion to date of the theological implications of recent neopragmatism and the new "historicist orientation in philosophy."[45] From several angles he shows the utter inadequacy of reducing the choice to that between certainty in the Cartesian agenda and despair at the failure of that agenda, or to the choice between a specific but irrelevant Christian identity and a relevant but faceless theology. In place of these dilemmas he suggests as a third option, theological history and community conversation.

But why in these cases was the option not forced? How could the pragmatist avoid subjectivism once all forms of metaphysical objectivism had been abandoned? Although the pragmatists do not directly answer this question, their implicit answer lies in their movement beyond dualism. Each of them rejects that sort of dualism which had earlier forced the eighteenth century British empiricists to separate the objective and value-free world known by the five senses from the subjective and value-laden world of speculation or emotion. Each of these pragmatists assumes that our ultimate context is a material *and* a valuable history, not a value-neutral matter standing beside a valuable spirit. And each of them argues that we have a way into the full dimensions of this material/valuable history: James by an affectional and bodily sensibility, West by a form of religious consciousness, and Lentricchia by the literary symbol. Consequently, when they reject dualism, they reject both objectivism and its ostensible alternative, subjectivism. When they accept a mind-body monism, they accept a third option, the possibility of discerning values in empirical history.

This is a peculiarly American pattern, found in variations of radical empiricism. Jonathan Edwards, James, Dewey, Whitehead, and the current school of process theologians and process philosophers, all affirmed that we have, in addition to the five senses, something analogous to a sixth sense. It is an affectional sensibility, added to the five senses, which enables us to experience values implicit in the objective world. Now it was just this radical empiricism which had led James to pragmatism, for radical empiricism had made both our experience and the world it experiences so confusing that we could never hope to find the truth through the method of correspondence. We had to move, then, to the pragmatic method, which would find the truth, not by seeking a clear correspondence between our belief and the external world, but by living in history, and testing our belief by seeing whether it offers the promised beneficial results. However, when it became evident that we had to decide what sort of results were beneficial, then pragmatism seemed hopelessly subjective, relative, and deeply arbitrary—for it had no extrahistorical criterion to say what counts as beneficial. But then, finally, it dawned that that was the problem of the dualist, not the problem of the American radical empiricist. Yes, if we begin with dualism, and if there are no values in history, then we are driven to merely subjective values. However, if we begin not with dualism, but with a radically empirical, matter/spirit monism, then there are values as well as facts in history, and pragmatism can test for values as well as facts. Consequently, an American pragmatist can hope that in historically testing options in the external world we might find non-subjective answers to the question of what counts as beneficial. This hope is what lies behind James's, West's, and Lentricchia's expectations that a socially active philosophy can keep us from hanging in a limbo.

According to James and Dewey, we were always already working with values, we had exercised the will to believe all along. As American empiricists they saw the universe as their value-laden home, rather than as an alien environment. William Clebsch in his *American Religious Thought* makes the case that this was a distinctly American gesture, involving not only those we are calling empirical liberals, but also those we are calling pietistic liberals. Further, Clebsch argues that seeing the universe as their home enabled Edwards, Emerson, and James to transform Protestantism and to move certain Americans from a preoccupation with moral ways of coping with the universe to a preoccupation with aesthetic ways of appreciating the universe.[46] Henry S. Levinson has extended Clebsch's type of analysis, claiming that Santayana also built his religious thought around such an aesthetic core.[47]

Finally then, in religion, the empirical religious liberals appropriated this valuational pragmatic answer theologically. They found a place to stand by citing their connection with the chain of biblical and ecclesiastical communities. Their use of this history gave them an external locus, thus moving them beyond subjectivism; at the same time their use of a radical empiricism gave them a value-laden history, thus moving them beyond a value-neutral objectivism. I refer specifically to members of the Chicago School of theology and to Douglas Clyde Macintosh of Yale, all of whom thought like pragmatists.[48] Shailer Mathews urged liberals to "approach religious problems from the point of view of the religious community," rather than from "a detached search for truth." This involved "the still more profound choice between religion as a form of social behavior rationalized and directed by intelligence, and religion as a philosophy in which the historical and social elements of an organized movement are to be ignored."[49] George Burman Foster, Gerald Birney Smith, Mathews, Case, Edward Scribner Ames, and others of the

Chicago School set forth a normative socio-historical method. They had no more patience with nornative indecision and formalism than James did, or West and Lentricchia do. This, then, allowed them to take a stand, to speak as Christians, even while they spoke as pragmatists (or, as they preferred, as "functionalists"), and prepared to test the utility of the Christian position.

Nevertheless, a latter-day empirical theologian like Bernard Meland might be so impressed with the pervasiveness of evil that for him the presence of good—not evil—is greeted as an incongruity.[50] Or Bernard Loomer, another latter-day empirical liberal, might find even God morally ambiguous.[51] Finally, as we said at the outset, it was clear all along that the empirical liberals could not move entirely beyond the tragic sense of life. For even if pragmatism could eliminate the uncertainty of historical obscurity and historical emergence (which it cannot), even if pragmatism could circumvent indecision in the effort to find a place to stand when talking about historical values (which it cannot), none of this meant that history and its failures could be escaped—as it could be escaped by the idealistic, fundamentalistic, or neo-orthodox critics of the "optimism" of the liberals.

Chapter 4

An Aesthetic Interpretation: The Elusive "It"

Logicians are not called in to advise artists. The key to the explanation is the understanding of the prehension of individuality. This is the feeling of each objective factor as an individual "It" with its own significance.[1]

No previous generation has been as acutely aware as we are that time ends. The importance of the extinction of the human species has come to overshadow the importance of the death of individuals. In the last hundred years we have confronted extinction by evolution's way of cutting down the species, extinction by the entropy of usable energy, and extinction by nuclear war. It is natural, then, for the present generation to seek value within the time which remains.

The question is, how? How is value in its full measure to be felt in the present? How is history's "it" to be discerned, if it is to be understood as Whitehead understood it above—as referring to the full amplitude of the individual object as it is known previous to rational elimination? Sensing the transitoriness of events, Whitehead declared that the day of judgment is always with us, and suggested that it is art's "business to render the day of judgment a success, now."[2] Concluding that the present worth of historical events is best felt prerationally, Whitehead suggested that history must be discerned aesthetically, as the artist discerns it.

The question then is, what must aesthetic experience be if it is to appreciate the full and present worth of history? For a generation aware that its time could end any time, this is an existential question of utmost importance.

For some earlier generations this appeared not to be a particularly important question. When Hebrew and Christian communities were conventionally eschatological in their view of history, then they could train their eyes on the terminus of history, and neglect the intrinsic importance of the present moment of history. Equally, when the Christians became Hellenized, they could train their eyes on the eternal, their true home now and in the future, and neglect the intrinsic importance of the present moment of history. These concerns of the Hebrews and the Christians usually eclipsed an interest in the aesthetic value of present history.

The temporal preoccupation of our generation resembles most closely that of the pre-eschatological Hebrews. Before the Babylonian exile in the sixth century B.C.E. the Hebrews looked to their immediate history, to God as active in that history, as the source of the value of their lives.

As with the pre-eschatological Hebrews, Whitehead looked to the search for the present worth of history as a religious quest—and he viewed that as the deeper reason for an aesthetic quest. Religion, according to Whitehead, contends "that the world is a mutually adjusted disposition of things, issuing in value for its own sake."[3] Implicitly, religion interprets that "value for its own sake" as aesthetic value, and seeks to discern the teleology of the universe, which is "directed to the production of Beauty."[4]

Finally, however, Whitehead affirmed that the quest for the present worth of history is not only aesthetic and religious; it is also empirical. It affirms that the full aesthetic amplitude of the "it" cannot be grasped except in a sensate mode. Speaking for American religious empiricism, Whitehead rejected the adequacy of the rational approach. When religious people, Whitehead said, "find their inspiration in their dogmas," well then, religions "commit suicide."[5] Dogmas represent abstractions; they substitute theories for experience, leaving behind what cannot be theoretically, or rationally, expressed.

Ironically, the most knowledgeable of the students of Whitehead have tended to couch Whitehead's aesthetic in rationalistic terms, and thus to vitiate the breadth of the empirical approach to aesthetic value. They have, in turn, neglected to say how the elusive "it" of history might be appreciated in the present moment.

I will in what follows: (1) describe the prevailing effort to develop a rationalistic Whiteheadian aesthetic; (2) describe the grounds for an empiricist Whiteheadian aesthetic; and (3) comment briefly on the religious importance of an empiricist aesthetic for American religious empiricism.

A Rationalistic Whiteheadian Aesthetic

In Whitehead's philosophy there are two ways of describing beauty, or aesthetic experience. Whitehead scholars, with damaging effects, have overemphasized one and underemphasized the other. They have so emphasized the rationalistic way, which concentrates on the intellectual organization of the past, that the meaning of aesthetic experience has been exaggerated. They have so underemphasized the empirical way, which concentrates on the physical response to the past, that the power of aesthetic experience has been neglected.

To state my point with greater intensity: the genius of the beautiful is its capacity to move us emotionally; when the Whitehead scholar accounts for the beautiful only rationalistically, much of this genius is missed. To say that aesthetic value can be comprehended rationally leaves out about as much as to say that Auschwitz can be comprehended as the misuse of freedom—in neither instance is the account incorrect; in both instances, when the account is the only account, the picture is distorted.

Donald W. Sherburne is the justly recognized foremost proponent of a rationalistic Whiteheadian aesthetic. His *A Whiteheadian Aesthetic* has subtly influenced numerous process philosophers and theologians.[6] Sherburne's rationalistic approach is embodied in his specific suggestion that for Whitehead an art work is a proposition or a part of a proposition and that aesthetic experience is a feeling of such a proposition. This approach is derived primarily from Whitehead's *Process and Reality*. A proposition proposes that certain select matters of fact, called "logical subjects," be interpreted, or theorized about, in terms of a particular "predicate." An art work embodies such a proposition (or, in the case of music, a predicative pattern only)[7] and the proposition (or its part) is the real meaning of the art, distinguishable from the physical artifact itself. The re-creation of this proposition in the conscious, definite, and intellectual awareness of the beholder is called a "propositional feeling," and it is this feeling which is aesthetic experience. This theory is rationalistic in that it identifies aesthetic experience with a clear, distinct, and ordered awareness of the external artistic reality.

Sherburne's rationalistic aesthetic conforms to a general approach long-standing in process thought. Both Whitehead and Charles Hartshorne have repeatedly argued that art and aesthetic experience arise within a structure of contrast within identity, or unity in variety.[8] This structure is suitable for ready apprehension by the mind, or the rationalizing self. The mind grips the beautiful, holds it within a category, sometimes called a proposition. This aesthetic rationality is, in turn, a remnant of the classical, Platonizing, and Cartesian effort of mentality to fasten onto the physical, to refuse to let the physical go until the physical has yielded some cognizable promise.[9]

On the other hand, from the empirical side, Whitehead and his colleagues in a radical empiricism, William James, Henri Bergson, and John Dewey have insisted that cognition is only an abstraction from the more fundamental physical experience, and that to treat the cognizable as the more real is—with a truly Cartesian forgetfulness—to put the wagon before the horse, to create a simulacrum. So, while those interpretations which stress contrast within identity and propositional meanings are by no means wrong, they are derivative and secondary, and should be treated accordingly.

It is only with regard to emphasis, then, that I am responding to talk of a rationalistic Whiteheadian aesthetic. Sherburne, for example, does include the empirical in his aesthetic analysis. He rejects the idealism of Benedetto Croce, and insists on the impor-

tance of the physical art object;[10] he rejects the "overintellectu-
alism" of Vernon Lee, and insists on the importance of
emotion.[11] Sherburne acknowledges that some art propositions
cannot be rendered linguistically; he acknowledges that art
propositions are first felt physically and that the function of
aesthetic experience is to bring clarity to the "vague and inarticulate feelings from a dim, penumbral region."[12] Nevertheless,
when Sherburne highlights Whitehead's specific accomplish-
ment, he chooses to take "very seriously" Whitehead's aim to
rescue the type of thought found in Bergson, James, and Dewey
"from the charge of anti-intellectualism." "An indispensable
step," Sherburne says, "in effecting his 'rescue' is the rationalization of 'the inner flux,' the giving to it of an intelligible structure." He maintains that Whitehead accomplishes this rationalization through a genetic analysis of conscious intellection.
Sherburne, in turn, claims that his own interpretation of Whitehead's aesthetic is "based on, not opposed to, that analysis of
conscious intellection."[13] Sherburne's aim is not to honor the
authenticity of the empirically immediate, "vague and inarticulate feelings from a dim, penumbral region." It is to rationalize,
clarify, and specify those feelings; it is, in short, to tame them. In
the area of aesthetics, it is to reduce them to a proposition, felt
with a propositional feeling.

As a proposition, the art object is about meaning, or theory;
it is something that may be said about events that may belong
together. From two sides it abstracts from brute actuality; it is an
imaginative predication about an imaginary selection of circumstances. The proposition lures the subject to simply recreate the
proposition in subjective experience. While the true art object is
real as an hypothesis is real, the physical artifact itself, whether a
thing (like a painting) or a performance, is only the medium
between the art hypothesis and the beholder's experience of the
hypothesis.

Now a rationalistic aesthetic is certainly not wrong, whether
in its interpretation of Whtiehead or of art. Any aesthetic which
eliminated entirely the propositional nature of art, reduced art to
something physical and aesthetic experience to a physical
encounter, would be silly. A piece of literature would be ink

scrawls on paper, and a great literary critic would be someone with an ocular affinity for black on white. Even if such preposterousness could be overcome, there would remain all of the questions of why perspective would not totally determine interpretation, as would happen if interactions were sheerly physical, and of how good art and good criticism would be distinguished from bad.[14] Clearly, art and its impact cannot be understood without some allowance for its status as an imaginative reality, a status deeply dependent on art's physicalness, but not reducible to physicalness.

Nevertheless, a rationalistic aesthetic fails to appreciate the aesthetic power of the experienced world. This is a criticism very difficult to sustain, for it refers to something beyond rationalization and, thus, beyond what can be expressed in a rationalistic argument. It could appeal to living memory, and question whether the love of art is finally a love of propositions, whether it is that much an affair of cognition. While an appeal to memory would be definitive in that, in a typically Whiteheadian fashion, it would refer "to the self-evidence of experience," at the same time it would refer to the vagaries of an entire life rather than to what can be held in a short exposition. Confined to a short exposition, I will fortify that exposition nevertheless, even as Whitehead did, by appeals to the world of events, to illustration, and to the history of philosophy.

An Empirical Whiteheadian Aesthetic

I have suggested that there are two sides to Whitehead's aesthetic, the rational and the empirical. Or, to state it more dramatically, there are two aesthetics, each mutually dependent on the other. While the rationalizing aesthetic emphasizes the intellectual organization of the world through propositions and propositional feelings, the empirical aesthetic emphasizes the immediate, physical, emotional, and nonconscious response to the world. An empirical aesthetic attempts to honor, rather than tame, those "vague and inarticulate feelings from a dim, penumbral region."

The importance of Whitehead's empirical aesthetic cannot

be understood apart from some discussion of Whitehead's notion of perception, and perception is best considered through a brief comment on Whitehead's notion of "symbolic reference" which, in turn, involves the notions of "causal efficacy" and "presentational immediacy." When the multiplicity of the past world physically and causally impinges on the body of the present subject, the world is felt only dimly, if at all consciously; the world is felt, Whitehead says, in its causal efficacy. The clear, fully conscious, and definite awareness of this world is a highly selective, abstract, and organized reduction of causal efficacy, giving a sense of an organized world there, in front of us, a sense Whitehead names presentational immediacy. The thousand physical influences of a green, warm, stale, almost-silent, lamp-lit, desk-furnished, late-at-night room are unconsciously eliminated in favor of a mental impression of a line read on the page on the desk before my eyes. We properly interpret that internal and mental impression of the line to refer to parts of the external and physical world of the room through a process Whitehead names symbolic reference. And quite commonsensically and pragmatically we regard the distinct, mental impression of the line as derivative from the physical impact of the world on our eyeballs. We do not—despite what David Hume and Immanuel Kant have said—finally regard our clear and distinct mental impressions as primary and nonderivative, and the world's causality as secondary and derived from the mind.[15]

While, Whitehead says, the clear, distinct, and conscious impressions of the mind are "handy" and provide "the manageable elements in our perceptions of the world," they are not what is most real or most important.[16] It is things which matter:

> But for all their vagueness, for all their lack of definition, these controlling presences, these sources of power, these things with an inner life, with their own richness of content, these beings, with the destiny of the world hidden in their natures, are what we want to know about.[17]

And we will know them better not by our clear and distinct impressions, but by our dim physical awareness, derivable from their initial impact on our bodies through causal efficacy.

To sense the world through causal efficacy is in essence, Whitehead says, to sense the aesthetic value of the world. It is to sense power at its deepest, and "the essence of power is the drive towards aesthetic worth for its own sake."[18] When Whitehead speaks of power this way, he recognizes that the *telos* of the universe is toward beauty, in that it aims toward the heightening of felt contrast. Consequently, the "sense of external reality— that is to say, the sense of being one actuality in a world of actualities—is the gift of aesthetic significance."[19]

This account of awareness is empirical because it is based on the immediate experience of the causal efficacy of the physical world; it is radically empirical because it claims to sense, in addition to the data for the five senses, the objective embodiments of values, and it senses these values "intuitively"—that is, physically —by, for example, a sense of aversion or a sense of attraction. Because, for Whitehead, those experienced values are essentially aesthetic values, this radical empiricism is aesthetic in orientation, and it can lead, in turn, to a developed, empirical aesthetic.[20]

An empirical aesthetic, when confronted with a rationalistic aesthetic, would claim that there are aesthetic objects other than propositions, for simply "the sense of being one actuality in a world of actualities" is an experience of something nonpropositional but aesthetic. Such experiences themselves are evidence for the further claim that there are more subjective aesthetic responses than those which can be called propositional feelings. Finally, an empirical aesthetic would claim, over against a rationalistic aesthetic, to be primary rather than secondary, necessary rather than accidental.[21] It would seek to bring to some dim awareness that intimate concourse of the body with the aesthetic worth of the world, and, somehow, in the process to preserve the immediacy of that concourse, as it is, prior to the abstraction of selected elements, the wholesale elimination of "irrelevancies," and the development of propositional feelings, all of which occur in a rational aesthetic judgment. An empirical aesthetic would seek to honor directly those "vast issues vaguely haunting the fullness of existence," to attend directly to that physical reaction to the world which says with incorrigible indefiniteness, " 'This is important,' 'That is different,' 'This is lovely.' "[22]

The greater comprehensiveness of an empiricist aesthetic can be illustrated by a reference to William Carlos Williams. For it is just this empirical sense of the aesthetic which distinguished Williams, particularly in his most conscious moments of rebellion from the cognitive and academic orientation of art. In his autobiography, in the midst of an explanation of how his work as a medical doctor facilitated his work as a poet, Williams said,

> I was permitted by my medical badge to follow the poor, defeated body into gulfs and grottos. And the astonishing thing is that at such times and in such places—foul as they may be with the stinking ischiorectal abscesses of our comings and goings— just there, the thing, in all its greatest beauty, may for a moment be freed to fly for a moment guiltily about the room. In illness, in the permission I as a physician have had to be present at deaths and births, at the tormented battles between daughter and diabolic mother, shattered by a gone brain—just there—for a split second—from one side or the other, it has fluttered before me for a moment, a phrase which I quickly write down on anything at hand, any piece of paper I can grab.[23]

This same radically empirical spirit is manifest in what may be Williams's most famous short poem, "The Red Wheelbarrow":

> So much depends
> upon
>
> a red wheel
> barrow
>
> glazed with rain
> water
>
> beside the white
> chickens.[24]

The "so much depends" is not the predicate of a proposition, but is an expression of the physical appreciation of a physical phenomenon—powerful, rich, and finally, inarticulate. The problem confronted by such a poem is not that of understanding, of explaining, or of establishing the rational relation among the logical subjects—wheelbarrow, rainwater, and white chickens. Rather, the problem is that of sheer relationality and facticity before one's eyes.[25] To regard such a poem as a proposition is to make it a banality; and for the Western scientifically minded academic intellectual, that is no trick at all.

A Religious Empiricist Aesthetic

To include the rationalistic aesthetic in an elaboration of Whitehead's thought is, as we have said, by no means wrong. But to single it out, even to the point of neglecting the empirical, is to fail to give Whitehead the proper intellectual lineage. It would be to make the father the child of the son; it would be to make Whitehead the child of his rationalist successors, like Charles Hartshorne, rather than to make Whitehead the child of Bergson and James and Dewey, all his philosophical antecedents and all radical empiricists in revolt against one form of rationalism or another.

Of course, these radical empiricists have their rationalistic side, as Whitehead does. John Dewey, even in his aesthetic, can be interpreted as a "propositionalist." In Art as Experience, it is valid to say that in one respect art is a proposition, suggesting a structure in terms of which an individual entity, already out of harmony with its environment, can achieve a new and harmonious relation with its environment.[26]

To say that alone, however, would be to distort Dewey, for it would leave the impression that art is the artist's rational construct, imposed on a world which lacks its own significance. Dewey, in fact, proceeds immediately to say,

> The live animal does not have to project emotions into the objects experienced. Nature is kind and hateful, bland and morose, irritating and comforting, long before she is mathematically qualified or even a congeries of "secondary" qualities like colors and their shapes.[27]

Accordingly and as a radical empiricist, Dewey places his emphasis on the discerment of objective value in the objective world. Dewey calls this value "quality," but by the term he means neither mathematical nor secondary qualities. He uses the term to refer, first, to the wholeness, or "deeper reality," in some aspect of the world, often as that wholeness is presented in a work of art.[28] If this were called the objective locus of quality, the subjective locus would be the emotional intuition of the objective quality. This subjective quality gives the experience itself the unity which makes it a particular experience.[29] It is this empirical discernment of quality which provides the substance of the derivative and propositional resolution of the conflict between the individual and its environment. So for Dewey the major aesthetic task is empirical; it is to discern properly the aesthetic quality of the external object.[30]

Whitehead's empiricist aesthetic is most evident in his *Symbolism* and *Modes of Thought*, where he reacts to Descartes's, Hume's, and Kant's trust in mental experience. They regarded the clear and distinct mental images of presentational immediacy as primitive, and causal efficacy as derivative. Whitehead calls this "a complete inversion of the evidence," and contends that it leads to the "fallacy of simple location" and the "fallacy of misplaced concreteness."[31] His response is, as we have said, to argue for the primitiveness of causal efficacy, and to contend that the primary aim of knowledge is to elucidate with as little abstraction as possible the immediacy of causal efficacy. This is a separate enterprise, quite different from the elucidation effected by presentational immediacy itself. In this empiricism, Whitehead should be regarded as a successor to Bergson, James, and Dewey, and not primarily as one who would correct their "anti-intellectualism."

The commonality among James, Bergson, Dewey, and Whitehead can be illustrated by reference to a curious linguistic move made by the three of those who were American. As we noted in the epigraph to this chapter, Whitehead in *Adventures of Ideas* said that the key to explanation "is the feeling of each objective factor as an individual 'It' with its own significance."[32] Why the inarticulateness, especially from Whitehead at his articulate best in what may be his most readable book? The answer may be that by using "It" in the way he does, he is attempting to point to a primal, physical, and immediate experience of objective value, an experience only vaguely and incompletely expressible through ordinary language. Virtually the same linguistic awkwardness appears in the writings of his American compatriots, James and Dewey. In *Essays in Radical Empiricism* James wrote,

> The instant field of the present is at all times what I call the "pure" experience. It is only virtually or potentially either object or subject as yet. For the time being, it is plain, unqualified actuality, or existence, a simple *that*.[33]

In *Art as Experience*, in his efforts to define that imperceptible "quality" in our experience of the immediate world, Dewey stumbles from language about having "*an* experience," to illustrations such as "*that was* an experience," and "*that* meal."[34] Bergson, however, chose simply to refer to sympathy and intuition, preferring, I suspect, understated Gallic style to awkward American ingenuousness.[35]

Their aesthetic approach sought to gain access to these "its" or "thats." But to accomplish this the aesthetics had to be empirical, not rationalistic. For these radically aestheticians, a rationalistic aesthetic is derivative, secondary, and indirect, merely the intellect's feeble effort to account for what in intellectual terms is unaccountable.

Now Whitehead, more than the others, extended this radically empiricist aesthetic into questions of religious experiences. He contended that the empirical alone approaches what is religiously complete. Whitehead contends that rationalistic religious arguments based on abstractions, such as the idea of perfection, depend upon "meaningless phrases respecting the unknown."[36] To get the totality of the divine, one must be open to bodily and affective experience. And this radically empirical perception is at base aesthetic—for what it perceives is "intrinsic importance for itself, for the others, and for the whole."[37]

When Whitehead advises that this empiricist aesthetic perceives intrinsic importance, or value for its own sake, in the history of religions and "in the intuitions of the finest types of religious lives," he is in full accord with William James. The genius and the heart of James's *The Varieties of Religious Experience* is its commitment to describing, one after another, the empirical particulars of numerous person's religious experiences, which were both empirical and aesthetic (producing immediate or remote delight).[38] The empirical challenge is taken up by such Chicago theologians as Shailer Mathews and Shirley Jackson Case as they examine testimonies from individuals and communities in biblical and ecclesiastical history. Bernard Meland and Bernard Loomer were later to note the specifically aesthetic dimensions of such historical and personal phenomena.

In short, an empiricist aesthetic ought to be able to point to the full measure of the vague and elusive religious values implicit in past history, and ought to be able to appreciate the intrinsic value in the present experience of that history. By comparison, a rationalistic aesthetic points to the derivative abstractions about past history, and, thereby, cannot appreciate the intrinsic value in the present experience of that history—despite the fact that the time for such experience is felt to be limited.

A question remains. While an empiricist aesthetic ought to be able to point to the obscure religious value in history, can it in fact accomplish that? If it is successfully to accomplish that, must it adopt a new form of theological expression, one more attuned to the religious value in history, a form of theology analogous to the form adopted in poetry by, say, William Carlos Williams?

Chapter 5

A Formal Interpretation: The Fate of an American Theology

The history of American religious empiricism presents a glaring incongruity. Spanning the work of Jonathan Edwards, of the more empirical of the Arminian and Unitarian clergy in the eighteenth and nineteenth centuries, of the liberal clergy and theologians in the last quarter of the nineteenth century and the first quarter of the twentieth century, up through the Chicago School of theology, to the process theology of our time, this history is representative of what George Santayana called "the genuine, the long silent American mind."[1] Yet, despite what would seem to be its natural appeal to the Americans in whose spirit it was written, American religious empiricism has been widely read only for brief interludes in the twentieth century, and it has been eclipsed by Continental forms of theology, particularly neo-orthodoxy and biblical hermeneutics.

Why has this happened? What might be done to enable the theology of American religious empiricism to find an American audience proportionate to what might be expected from its distinctly American content?

Noting a similar anomaly, Donald H. Meyer suggested that the source of neglect might be a failure of theological form.

Asking why "American religious humanism" had failed to capture a popular audience, Meyer contended that it was written in a rational, abstract form which kept it from offering "emotional nourishment for the average person."[2]

Adopting a tactic similar to Meyer's, I will argue that theological empiricism failed to capture a larger theological audience because it seldom utilized a theological form capable of expressing its historicist content. It was written in an abstract form, quite suitable for the dogmatic theology of a Karl Barth or the idealistic theology of a Paul Tillich, but generally incapable of giving the reader a sense of the concrete and affective contents which were the primary data for theological empiricists. As a result, one virtually had to have studied with an empirical theologian to have a feel for theological empiricism.

I will argue this case by analogy: the poet, William Carlos Williams, adopted the point of view held by American religious empiricism, and represented the same "genuine, the long silent American mind." However, he felt it was necessary to develop a new poetic form to enable him to express the concrete and affective contents primary in his own empiricism. This seemed to have worked, for Williams was enormously effective in persuading the community of poets to take seriously and even to adopt his poetry of American empiricism. Using the analogy offered by Williams, I will suggest that American empirical theologians should adopt a theological form appropriate to their historicist content, enabling the American community of theologians better to utilize the empirical content and the empirical method to which they are naturally heir.

Two Literary Efforts

The second and enlarged 1921 edition of Karl Barth's *The Epistle to the Romans* became, in Karl Adam's words, a "bombshell on the playground of the theologians."[3] Just a year later Eliot published *The Waste Land*. William Carlos Williams, standing on the playground of the poets, called it "the great catastrophe to our letters."[4]

Barth and Eliot greeted the chaos of their time by exalting

the sacred canon. That Barth found in his canon the word of God and Eliot did not, was simply a question of personal style. The two canons worked out of the same premise: the issues of the present should be answered with the texts of the past. But to those interested in answers generated out of an empirical history rather than a static text, this is a destructive hypothesis.

The enormity of the canonizer's impact and its pathetic aftermath in America may be better depicted by Williams in his comments on poetry than it is by any theologian commenting on theology. Williams said: "There was heat in us, a core and a drive that was gathering headway upon the theme of a rediscovery of a primary impetus, the elementary principle of all art, in the local conditions. Our work staggered to a halt for a moment under the blast of Eliot's genius, which gave the poem back to the academics. We did not know how to answer him."[5]

The empirical theologian can learn from Williams. There was for Williams a new and local possibility, there was a proper loyalty to that possibility and a collaboration in that loyalty. And there was a willingness to challenge those who ignore that possibility. Just then in America an experiment was getting underway. It rejected the Kantian isolation of the human subject from the external world, as well as the Platonic separation of the mind from the body, as well as the aristocratic elevation of the lettered above the unlettered. It affirmed the inseparability of subject and world, of what we call spirit from what we call matter, and of the elite from the common. It grew out of American history, a history highlighted in Williams's *In the American Grain*. And it claimed that local history was the best place to find what is of general importance.

According to Williams, Eliot was a traitor to the American possibility because he adopted as his referents, not local, physical, or ordinary history, but the great remote literary creations of the human spirit. Eliot went to Europe and wrote poems like *The Waste Land*, which had to be footnoted.

Williams's rejection of Eliot derived from Williams's loyalty to an American epistemology. He expressed this epistemology in his phrase, "no ideas but in things," which summarized his position on two fronts. First, it said implicitly, "no ideas

in ideas," no ideas arise from ideas; thereby it denied epistemological idealism in general, and the scholarly predilection in
particular. "The position of the mind is *outside* all categories,"[6]
said Williams. Second, Williams's motto affirmed empiricism,
claiming that ideas arise from the experience of things—meaning
objects, events and relations in the world of embodiment. The
very word "artist" meant for Williams "nearly this thing alone":
one who rigorously maintains "contact with an immediate objective world of actual experience."[7]

When Williams placed himself against idealism and with
empiricism, however, he qualified his empiricism, making it a
radical empiricism. Williams sought "to understand the meaning
of knowledge" and rejected that empirical positivism which
would "brutalize" and "dwarf" the reader in "a sleet of information."[8] To move beyond a positivistic empiricism in order to
adopt an inclusive, value-perceiving, and radical empiricism, one
must exercise imagination and a bodily awareness.[9]

Again, this was for Williams no mere debating point. It was
a stance toward knowing mandated by a post-modern set of
implications just then emerging in the sciences as well as in the
arts. To live in the twentieth century, particularly in America,
and to turn your back on these mandates was a betrayal of the
mission of the poet; it was a poetic lie, and it was a cheat to those
people who need a poetry which addresses their own world.

For Williams the nub of the problem was the development
of a poetic form capable of receiving and conveying the fuller
history presupposed by radical empiricism. Poetry, in short,
must be reconceived if it is really to convey history, where
history is not a hieratic sequence of elite spiritual artifacts, but is
things as well as ideas, bodies as well as minds, the ordinary as
well as the extraordinary, the value-laden as well as the value-
free, the local as well as the global. The poetic line must be
remade if, somehow, it is to capture that history and to commun-
icate it to the reader.

Williams was insistent. He intended to be a poet whose
poetry arises "from the society about him of which he is (if he is
to be fed) a part," and not a poet who writes and thinks "in terms
of a direct descent of great minds,"[10] nor a poet who creates a

product to be regarded in and for itself. Rather, Williams treated the poem as a process, receiving from the surrounding society and then communicating the poet's interpretation back to the society. For Williams the poem was a projectile, from the society to the poet, from the poet back to society.

Williams's stance in all this is relevant to a second literary effort, American empirical theology, because Williams was working out of the same American embodiment and making many of the same interpretations as were the empirical theologians. Williams's stance is instructive to the theologian because he and his fellow poets were somehow able to hold their own against the other side of their community, while the American theologians were not.

If there is a tip to the American iceberg on which both Williams and the empirical theologians stood, it is the philosophy of Alfred North Whitehead. Of course, it is odd to call Whitehead, an Englishman moved to America, the obvious common American ancestor. But then, Whitehead was to America as Eliot was to England—a native son by temperament, if not by birth. Had Whitehead been an Englishman by temperament he would have held to David Hume, not made him his principal antagonist. Hume, in his search for certainty, had denied the reliability of all that was not an idea related to ideas or a conscious report of one of the five senses. He denied that so-called experiences of values were accurate comments on the world. From Whitehead's American standpoint it can be said that Hume, with a British delicacy, shunned the clammier, darker bottom stories of experience, and avoided thereby the more primitive, bodily, and affectional perceptions from which our experience of value arises. As we have noted earlier, Whitehead, like Dewey and James and the liberal nineteenth century clergy and Jonathan Edwards before him, was equipped with a naivete which allowed him to accept as sometimes reliable the reports of those who claimed to experience objective values. And yet Whitehead acknowledged the elusive nature of objective values, calling them "unmanageable, vague, and ill-defined."[11]

Of Whitehead's *Science and the Modern World* Williams says, "Finished reading it at sea, September 26, 1927—A milestone surely in my career, should I have the force and imagination to go on with work."[12] It has been noted that "about that time varieties of the term 'objectivist' began to appear important in Williams's prose,"[13] and that Whitehead's realism provided "a philosophic base for Williams's credo 'no ideas but things.' "[14]

Now Williams and the American empirical theologians agree in principle that the prime objective is to get to the primitive experience which Whitehead and his American ancestors had emphasized. Whitehead, in particular, had seen how gaining access to that experience involves both religion and poetry. Religion should be the effort to move beneath clear and distinct data, to perceive the primitive values within our social history. Finally, for Whitehead "religion is world loyalty."[15] Yet Whitehead recognized that even in America this theological orientation had not been established. He contended that "the real, practical problems of religion had never been adequately studied in the only way in which such problems *can* be studied, namely, in the school of experience."[16] It is here that poetry is important, for poetry is an ideal instrument for gaining access to such primitive experience. At the beginning of his American career Whitehead said, "I hold that the ultimate appeal is to naive experience, and that is why I lay such stress on the evidence of poetry."[17] At the end of his career he said, "Philosophy is akin to poetry, and both of them seek to express that ultimate good sense which we term civilization."[18]

It is my contention that Williams pursued this Whiteheadian and American mandate more successfully than did the theologians. Randall Jarrell, referring to this empirical character of Williams's mission, said that Williams is so "American that the adjective itself seems inadequate . . . one exclaims in despair and delight: He is the America of poets."[19] Williams was the first American poet to move his writing to a position beyond subject-object dualism.[20] Most important, Williams followed through on this content by adopting a poetic form he thought was capable of conveying the affective content of his local world. It was this form which heavily influenced poets such as Charles Olson, Allen Ginsberg, Robert Creeley, Gary Snyder, Theodore Roethke, David Ignatow, and Denise Levertov. This and related events mounted, until in 1979 Ekbert Faas, in his *Towards A New American Poetics*, could refer to the "ascendence of a new art and aesthetics over the Eliot-dominated New Critical literary hierarchy which still controls most universities."[21]

By contrast, the American empirical theologians began early and faded early—but not completely. This tradition—stretching from Edwards, thinning through the nineteenth century, thickening with the liberals toward the end of the nineteenth century, thickening more with James, Dewey, Whitehead and the empirical theologians, especially of the Chicago School; then (with the onslaught of neo-orthodoxy) becoming thin again in the mid-twentieth century—suggests a failure, contrasting with Williams's success.

There are, however, developments on the horizon which together indicate a potential for the restoration of an American religious empiricism. William J. Hynes cites new signs of interest in the Chicago School in his recent *Shirley Jackson Case and the Chicago School*.[22] There is evidence that the process theologians are newly interested in the social sciences, emphasizing the empirical side of Whitehead's heritage more and the metaphysical, rationalistic side less.[23] Cornel West, first at Union Theological Seminary, now at Yale Divinity School, is introducing neo-pragmatist thought into religious studies, as well as connecting this stream of thought to Afro-American experience.[24] The new *American Journal of Theology and Philosophy* is dedicated to reviving themes of relevance to American religious liberalism and to the Chicago School of theology. None of these developments, however, indicates the success of American empirical theology, particularly a success which would fulfill its enormous original potential.

Robert Funk, in his 1975 presidential address before the Society of Biblical Literature has indicated how major the loss of the distinctly American theological emphasis has been—at least in one area, biblical scholarship. The socio-historical method of biblical criticism developed by Ernest DeWitt Burton, Shailer Mathews, and Shirley Jackson Case was a direct challenge to the literary method preferred by William Rainey Harper, a biblical scholar from Yale and the first president of the University of

Chicago. Harper sought to introduce the German methods of higher criticism, with their concentration on biblical languages, textual criticism, grammar, lexicography, verse-by-verse interpretation, and translation. The irony was that the experiential emphasis of Burton, Mathews, and Case won temporarily at Chicago but lost in the world of American biblical scholarship, while the literary emphasis of Harper lost temporarily at Chicago, but came to prevail in the increasingly literary-hermeneutical world of American biblical scholarship. Even though the method of the Chicago School successfully anticipated, Funk says, "the emerging common consciousness"[25] of the twentieth century and was the "index to common American consciousness,"[26] in its role as an alternative to the literary approach it "disappeared from the record as though it never took place."[27]

For our purposes, the irony is heightened when it is realized that the prevailing literary-hermeneutical methods of biblical criticism imply a formalism and a commitment to the textual canon which generally correspond to the methods of T. S. Eliot and Karl Barth. For in each case the great spiritual literature and its mandate is considered primarily in itself; in each case the local and the empirical are quite secondary. In American theology empirical historicism has had, at best, a muted success, and its opponent has won royally.

The contrast with Williams's success in the world of poetry is vivid.

William Carlos Williams's Poetic Form

Williams may have been successful in moving so many American poets in the direction of a historicist poetry because he went beyond talking about the mere theory of the poem as an embodiment of historical realities, to utilizing a form capable of conveying the concrete and affective content of a living historical situation—particularly in the 246-page *Paterson*. Williams did begin to attain national prominence only after the serial publication of the five books of *Paterson* was initiated in 1946. So it is natural to surmise that it was the poetic form of *Paterson* which fundamentally enhanced Williams's persuasiveness.

Williams's poems previous to *Paterson* often had been imagist or objectivist efforts to provide glimpses or empirical snapshots of particular scenes or situations. But then, with references to his writing of *Paterson*, Williams says, "The longer I lived in my place, among the details of my life, I realized that these isolated observations needed pulling together to gain 'profundity,' "[28] He contends that *Paterson* is "an assertion, always, of a new and total culture; the lifting of an environment to expression."[29] In another context he speaks like a true radical empiricist when he defines culture as "the realization of the qualities of a place in relation to the life which occupies it."[30] At bottom, then, *Paterson* was written as an historicist poem, an effort to express the culture of Paterson, New Jersey.

Williams faulted those poets who ignore "the direct application of American culture,"[31] the "specific study of American tendencies."[32] So in *Paterson*, Williams styles himself as one who would stay behind in America after "the rest have run out— /after the rabbits," as one who, like a lame dog, would embark upon the humble empirical examination of America, who would "Deceive and eat. Dig/a musty bone."[33] *Paterson* is Williams's American and empirical counterpart to *The Cantos* and *The Waste Land*, the great poems of two Americans who ran out, Ezra Pound and T. S. Eliot.

The specifically formal challenge of *Paterson* was to develop a style and a poetic line capable of capturing the history and culture of Paterson, New Jersey, and of conveying it to the reader. His intention was to treat the city directly, attempting always to avoid the scholarly tendency of relating to things only "intermediately through thought."[34] In serving this end, Williams, like the American radical empiricists before him, was sincere to the point of risking the appearance of naivete. He knew a reversion to the styles and ideas of the great literature of the European past would gain him entry to the academy and to the world of literary fashion, where then he was often scorned. But when he said "no ideas but in things," he felt, as did the American composer, Charles Ives, that it was his obligation to sing the songs which were actually sung in his presence, not refurbish the great inherited art. So, for example, when history was accidental and random, then the poetry commenting on history should be aleatory in form. The form of poetry, in short, must arise from the forms of experienced history. Paul Mariani in his *William Carlos Williams: A New World Naked* aptly describes Williams's historicist concern when he says, "By order he meant a pattern discovered in the world, from things as they were, like (says Williams) 'the newspaper that takes things as it finds them— mutilated and deformed.' "[35]

It is a poetry which shuns the predetermined, traditional line, even the premeditated line of free verse. It is written with a "variable foot," a foot varying according to the lengths of the actual, spoken phrasing of the American idiom.

In its content *Paterson* claims that the city is marked by the failure of love, by divorce, but also that it shows signs of a new love, a new marriage. The waterfalls at Paterson tell it all: there is an original gathering of the waters, then a dispersion as the waters fall, and then there should be a regathering at the bottom of the falls. The evil is that the natural dispersion has become an unnatural divorce; the unnatural task of the poet is to discover that new human response which will create out of this divorce a new marriage.

Books I, II, and most of III detail evidence of divorce in Paterson and, in effect, in contemporary America. A local stuntman, famous for jumping from the top of the falls into the water below, left home, lost touch with Paterson, and on his return attempted to repeat his feat, but was killed at the bottom of the falls. A doctor, groups of boys, academics, evangelists, and various capitalists all fail to promote true marriage with their context, to create anything but an increasingly aggravated divorce. Language has gone awry. "Love is no comforter, rather a nail in the skull."[36] What is needed is a poet who can stand at the bottom of the falls, listen to "the roar of the present," and discover a new and reconciling language,[37] to induce a new and reconciling love.

The central image of hope is Madame Curie discovering radium: "A dissonance/in the valence of Uranium/led to the discovery/Dissonance/(if you are interested)/leads to discovery."[38] Madame Curie confronted dissonance in all its concreteness and in that dissonance she discovered a new possibility: "a stain at the bottom of the retort/without weight, a failure, a/nothing. And then, returning in the night to find it/LUMINOUS!"[39]

Following the mandate of Curie, *Paterson* derives a formal answer: one must split the explicit sentence, and with that fission, that breaking into verbal sequences, that return to things in all their disparate localness, there will be released the energy of love, of new ideas, which will foster new marriage, a new poetic form. The form of the poem imitates and thereby conveys its content. And it is this more positive note, both about the world and the form of *Paterson* which then is developed in the last books of the poem.

Paterson's content is capable also of a religious reading. That in Paterson dissonance leads to discovery is inexplicable; it could have been otherwise, but that it was not makes all the difference. Divorce, with an entropic inexorability, could lead always to destruction, to devolution. Instead, sometimes it can be seen as creative discord, as a dissonance leading to a new fusion, a new marriage, an unexpected evolution. Objectively there is an inexplicable tropism towards new forms of marriage, and it is working in Paterson, in history. It is not invented by the poetic ego, it is not borrowed from high culture, it is not rationalized from the thin air of eternal ideas. It is discovered to be active in history. And it can be discovered and received by one who faithfully and empirically returns to the particulars, to "the roar of the now."

In this empiricism Williams is following Whitehead's recommendation that religion attend the school of experience, that it act out of world loyalty. Equally, Williams's history-listening echoes the Old Testament prophet's history-listening; each points towards what William James called "a More."

Paterson's historicism and its form collaborate to bring the reader slowly to feel divorce in Paterson, New Jersey, as well as the possibility of new marriage. Out of the welter of circumstances set end-to-end, out of the images, the excerpts from actual letters and newspaper stories and history books, the explanations by the poet of his intentions in writing what is being written, and the "Deformed verse . . . suited to deformed morality,"[40] something can happen to the reader. He or she can begin, slowly and uncannily, to feel the emotional content of the history set forth in the poem. Apart from this form and its effect, Paterson is just so much poetic experimentation. Apart from this, the art of Paterson is missed, the profundity, the quality, the patersonian culture is missed. But with this, the reader can experience recent American history newly.

Empirical Theology and a New Form

American empirical theology might be effectively revived if it learns, as Williams did, to convey through its form the valuational depths of history. This hypothesis is supported with the analogy of William Carlos Williams, whose poetic form in Paterson conveys a sense of the local, its randomness, its emotion, and its saturation in the values of alienation and love. This hypothesis is further supported through the use of certain correlations: between Williams's relative success in persuading the community of poets and his empirical form in poetry, and between the empirical theologians' relative failure in persuading the community of theologians and their lack of an empirical form in theology.

Given the possibility that a new theological form might permit American empirical theology to be more effective, it seems important to ask what that form might be.

Charles Olson's historicist comments on poetic form provide important guidance in a search for a specific, new theological form for empirical theology. Olson, a poet who studied and lectured on Whitehead, developed a theory of "projective verse" which Williams quoted extensively in his autobiography. Olson said that projective poetry is marked by: (1) kinetics: "a poem is energy transformed from where the poet got it . . . , by way of the poem itself to, all the way over to, the reader"; (2) principle: "FORM IS NEVER MORE THAN AN EXTENSION OF CONTENT"; and (3) process: "ONE PERCEPTION MUST IMMEDIATELY AND DIRECTLY LEAD TO A FURTHER

PERCEPTION."[41] Projective poetry aims to work in direct contact with the flow of natural and social history. Form must follow content; only thereby can it project the values of the world all the way over to the reader, and further, convey the sense of the development of those values.

To put it another way, American empirical theology cannot escape the mandate that it become in form a "process theology." What is typically called process theology is called that primarily for reasons of content; the theology is dependent on the process metaphysics of Alfred North Whitehead. Here, however, I want to discuss a process theology named for its form. Donald Kartiganer makes an analogous point in an article entitled, "Process and Product: A Study of Modern Literary Form." He argues that product literature is written to present a literary entity which will stand on its own, confront the world with an order, and thereby answer the chaos of the world. Process literature does not begin by treating the world as chaos, in need of structure. It begins with a version of the world best described, Kartiganer says, by Henri Bergson. For Bergson "reality must be seen as a continuous becoming, and literature must try to reflect life as this 'continuous creation of unforeseeable novelty.' "[42] When we impose preconceived literary schemes on the world, says Bergson, we fail to represent this creative motion. What we should do, he says, is to adopt "supple, mobile, and almost fluid representations, always ready to mould themselves on the fleeting forms of intuition."[43] Kartiganer extends this point, saying that process literature has the aim "of duplicating the constant movement of nature, of shattering the discrepancies between the intensity of raw experience and its transformation into verbal form."[44] The proximity to the world of raw experience is taken so seriously by some writers of process literature that in their writing they include efforts to describe their own experience with the world about which they are writing.

Kartiganer takes as the prime example of process literature Williams's *Paterson*. We can put our question by asking whether something like the precedent set by Williams can be extended to American empirical theology. Can there be in the theology appropriate to American religious empiricism something like what John Cobb found in the form of Marjorie Suchocki's process theology: "Her style is appropriate to what she says. It moves and flows, and it unites thought and feeling."[45]

Obviously, there is no single literary form best suited to American empirical theology. And among the forms possibly suggested for that theology, none should require that the theologian become a poet, although they can require that the theologian become artful—as good scholars always have been. For, whatever the form, an artfulness is required if the theologian is both to sense the religious dimension of historical experience, and to use form deliberately in an effort to convey the affective meaning of religious history.

I would name, as one possible literary form appropriate to American empirical theology, the form of the interpreting historian. A theologian as an interpreting historian is an historian, and writes about religious individuals, religious thinkers, and religious communities of the past; but as an interpreter this theologian reads the past in a way that makes it pragmatically useful for a present community. Such a theologian is not animated primarily by the intention to formulate a rationally necessary system, or to state a doctrine which captures a biblical, an ecclesiastical, or a traditional truth for all times and places. An interpreting historian is, above all, loyal to a specific communal past, but is willing independently to interpret that past for a specific contemporary community. An interpreting historian is an interpreter—one who advances the free response of a present individual or community to a particular past. But also, an interpreting historian is an historian—one who recognizes the present's dependence on the power of the past and also on the unavoidable fact that the past restricts the range of possible present interpretations.

The image of the interpreting historian indicates a more specific theological form than might at first appear. Because the interpreting historian must regard a specific history and suggest a specific interpretation of that history, the form of writing must be concrete. This contrasts to the theologian who seeks an uninterpreted and objective truth, a truth which is true precisely because it is sufficiently abstract to apply to all times and places.

The interpreting historian, like Derrida, would seek to forge a current link in the chain of past interpretations. But unlike some formalistic and subjectivistic American deconstructionist literary critics, the interpreting historian would seek to avoid an interpretation which sought, more than anything else, to be expressive. Like Carl Becker, who in 1932 wrote *Every Man His Own Historian*, the interpreting historian would recognize that every person is his or her own historian, but recognizes also that every person also is a member of the past. Like Alfred North Whitehead, the interpreting historian seeks to capture by an empirical attentiveness the elusive "it" of the past, but to accomplish this for the present.

Bernard Loomer's notion of "size," discussed in Chapter 1, offers a possible criterion for the interpreting historian. Recognizing that there is a range of conceivable interpretations of the past, Loomer named "size" as a measure for selecting the best interpretation. The interpretation with greatest size is the interpretation which includes historical experiences so diverse, appreciations of history so wide-ranging, that it stops just short of being so inclusive, so filled with the ambiguities of natural and human behavior, that it would destroy the integrity, the unity, the sanity of the interpreting individual or community. Loomer proposed that Jesus accomplished that for his time and community, and that that was what made him the Christ.[46] Loomer suggested that in his ministry and in his death Jesus opened himself in love to the strengths and the evils of those around him, and for his own community brought these diverse voices into a meaningful whole. As a criterion, size would suggest an ideal indicating which interpretation, within the range of possible interpretations, is best.

The form of Frank Lentricchia's *Criticism and Social Change* could serve as a model for the form of an American empirical theology. Lentricchia offers a theory of literary criticism, but presents it as an interpretation for our own time of the life and writings of Kenneth Burke. Lentricchia's effort is interpretive, not only in its treatment of Burke, not only in its juxtaposition of Burke to Paul de Man and to contemporary trends in literary criticism, but in its application to current social needs. And

Lentricchia's interpretation is a disturbing interpretation, one with size.

The historians of the Hebrew Bible and of the Synoptic Gospels, those described in the "Introduction" of this book, may provide the most viable model for the form of American empirical theologians. Gerhard von Rad, it will be remembered, through his notion of tradition history brought to the attention of the community of biblical scholars the fact that much of the Hebrew Bible had a particular form: it is a series of reinterpretations of the crucial events in the life of the Hebrew people. In his 1938 essay, "The Form-Critical Problem of the Hexateuch," von Rad argued that the Hexateuch is a series of ever-expanding, always-updated, re-expressions of the meaning of those events from the Exodus through the Settlement.[47] The interpretations were created to meet the problems of new social locations and new times, and in that creation the Hebrew faith was created. In his 1957 *Old Testament Theology*, von Rad extended his thesis, applying it beyond the Hexateuch.[48] Twenty years later *Tradition and Theology in the Old Testament*, an anthology edited by Douglas Knight, brought von Rad's tradition history into conversation with current problems of biblical hermeneutics. In that anthology Robert B. Laurin argues that the early Christian church's use of the Hebrew scriptures extends the tradition history method of the writers of the Hebrew Bible into the writing of the New Testament. These and similar discussions by biblical scholars show how many of the writers of the Bible are interpreting historians. They literally created the faith through their construction of a chain of interpretations of their history and of its central figures.

The new sociologists of the Bible offer a similar model for the form of the interpreting historian. Norman Gottwald's *The Tribes of Israel: A Sociology of the Religion of Liberated Israel, 1250–1050*, John G. Gager's *Kingdom and Community: An Anthropological Approach to Civilization*, and Wayne Meek's *The First Urban Christians: The Social World of the Apostle Paul* demonstrate a sociological (or anthropological) approach to the Bible. Gottwald, Robin Scroggs in studies of the New Testament, and several other biblical scholars have extended the sociological approach, offering a model for the writing of a theology for current times. In *The Bible and Liberation: Political and Social Hermeneutics* not only do they see the biblical writers as interpreting the social struggles of their time, but they argue that the most appropriate response to this history of struggle is for us to interpret the Bible in such a way that it calls for an extension of the struggle into the present. They see current liberation theology as one way to extend this struggle.

Now the point is that these biblical scholars have functioned as interpreting historians. Most of them accomplish their task modestly, by seeing the biblical writers as interpreting historians, and leaving implicit the notion that a current biblical faith would be faithful to these ancient historians by using their form as a mandate for present form. The sociological biblical scholars who are liberation theologians more boldly spell out a current interpretation of the biblical writer's interpretations. While the particular Marxist cast to their thought could well be challenged, they have practiced a form appropriate to the interpreting historian. And, not incidentally, their efforts (by and large without acknowledgement) emulate the socio-historical methods of the Chicago School biblical scholars, Shailer Mathews and Shirley Jackson Case. The Chicago School socio-historical method required both: 1) the analysis of the biblical characters and communities in the context of their own history, and 2) a reinterpretation of the writings of these characters and communities for our own time.

The form appropriate for the interpreting historian is implicit in the foregoing. It lies in describing religious writings as interpretations of their historical context, and in reinterpreting those writings for one's own time. This form must be concrete, in that it tells of particular events and does it for particular times and places.

But it might be asked how such historical commentary will ever carry the affective meaning, the evocative power that, say, William Carlos Williams called forth in his poetic rendering of Paterson, New Jersey. How could such historical commentary ever reveal the elusive "it" appropriate to a radically empirical approach? Of course, there is no simple response to these challenges. Nevertheless, the valuational depths of history might be evoked by an imaginative use of interpretive history. For example, a narrative of a religious figure, of his or her conflicts, struggles, and responses, might evoke a sense of the values once felt and exercised by that person. Or, a narrative which interpreted such a figure by showing the challenge which he or she posed for the contemporary reader might evoke a sense of current history's religious values. I would conclude that that is exactly why the biblical stories reveal values in the past and challenge the values of each generation of readers. I think that that is why the more narrative efforts at theology in the past have had a more-than-cognitive impact.

The student of American religious empiricism, in short, might become an interpreting historian. American empirical theology might assume the form of an interpretive religious history, focusing on the narrative reinterpretation of a chain of religious thinkers. Well executed, this form might evoke in the reader an empirical feel for the divine struggle within the history of the past and of the present.

Notes

Preface

1. Sydney E. Ahlstrom, *Theology in America: The Major Protestant Voices from Puritanism to Neo-Orthodoxy* (Indianapolis: The Bobbs-Merrill Co., Inc., 1967), p. 23.

2. For a good introduction, see John B. Cobb, Jr. and David Griffin, *Process Theology: An Introductory Exposition* (Philadelphia: Westminster Press, 1976).

3. Bruce Kuklick, *The Rise of American Philosophy: Cambridge, Massachusetts, 1860-1930* (Yale University Press: New Haven, 1977), p. xxvi.

Introduction: The Context of American Religious Empiricism

1. William James, "The Will to Believe," in *The Will to Believe and Other Essays, Popular Philosophy and Human Immortality: Two Supposed Objections to the Doctrine* (New York: Dover Publications, 1956), p. 52.

2. Daniel D. Williams, "Tradition and Experience in American Theology," in *The Shaping of American Religion*, ed. by James Ward Smith and A. Leland Jackson (Princeton, NJ: Princeton University Press, 1961), p. 459.

3. Ibid., p. 473.

4. Gerhard von Rad, *The Theology of Israel's Historical Traditions*, Vol. 1: *Old Testament Theology*, translated by D.M.G. Stalker (New

York: Harper and Brothers, 1962), p. 138. See also Gerhard von Rad, *Wisdom in Israel* (Nashville and New York: Abingdon Press, 1977), especially Chapter 9, "The Self-Revelation of Creation."

5. Von Rad, *Old Testament Theology*, p. vi.

6. Gerhard von Rad, "The Form-Critical Problem of the Hexateuch," in *The Problem of the Hexateuch and Other Essays* (New York: McGraw-Hill Book Company, 1955).

7. Von Rad, *Old Testament Theology*, pp. 105–109.

8. Robert B. Laurin, "Tradition and Canon," in *Tradition and Theology in the Old Testament*, ed. by Douglas A. Knight (Philadelphia: Fortress Press, 1977), p. 272.

9. Ibid., 266–267.

10. Douglas A. Knight, "Revelation through Tradition," in *Tradition and Theology*, p. 169.

11. This distinction between pietistic liberals and empirical liberals diverges, it should be noted, from other efforts to establish the two types of liberals. In his *The Modernist Impulse in American Protestantism* (New York: Oxford University Press, 1982, p. 7) William R. Hutchinson notes the "common way of categorizing different types of liberal," which was

> to assume that the difference between "modernists" and "evangelical liberals" was a difference of starting points and of fundamental loyalties. An "evangelical liberal" was alleged to have been a religious thinker who made the Christian revelation normative and then merely interpreted it in the light of modern knowledge. A "modernistic liberal," on the other hand, was said to have been someone who had made modern science his criterion and then, in a kind of afterthought, retained what he could of the Christian tradition. (p. 7)

Such a categorization by starting points and loyalties is found in Kenneth Cauthen"s *The Impact of American Religious Liberalism* (New York: Harper and Row, 1962), pp. 13 and 15, and Henry P. Van Dusen's *The Vindication of Liberal Theology* (New York: Charles Scribner's Sons, 1963), pp. 23–25. The terms "evangelical liberal" and "modernist" point to generally the same people to which my "pietistic liberal" and "empirical liberal," in that order, point. Hutchinson properly rejects, however, the rationale behind the common categorization, saying that it tends to honor just that secular/sacred division which all liberals "sought to minimize." Hutchinson quotes Theodore Munger, a liberal of the 1880s, who said, "The New Theology does indeed regard with question the line often drawn between the sacred and the secular—a line not to be found in Jewish or Christian Scriptures, nor in man's nature" (Hutchinson, *Modernist Impulse*, p. 8). Hutchinson, in short, places the unity of the secular and the sacred at the heart of liberalism, and with this I am in agreement. I have attempted, however, to augment Hutchinson's point by reintroducing rough equivalents to the evangelical and modernist liberals, and contending that one, the pietistic liberals, found a unity of the secular and the sacred only in human experience, and that the other, the empirical liberals, found that unity both in human experience and in the world to which that experience refers.

12. In this interpretation I am guided by G. J. Warnock, "Kant," in *A Critical History of Western Philosophy*, ed. by D. J. O'Connor (New York: The Free Press, 1964), pp. 296–318.

13. Over halfway through *The Dynamics of Faith* Tillich notes that "everything said about faith in the previous chapters is derived from the experience of actual faith" (New York: Harper & Row, Publishers, 1957), p. 99. In that most representative of his books Tillich derives from faith even the criterion for the ultimacy (the divinity) of the God of faith.

14. Tillich, *Dynamics*, p. 49.

15. Henry F. May, *The Enlightenment in America* (New York: Oxford University Press, 1979), p. xiv.

16. This is to accept Perry Miller's interpretation of Edwards as a Lockean; see Chapter 1 below.

17. See the discussion of James's rejection of Spencer in Jacques Barzun, *A Stroll with William James* (New York: Harper and Row, Publishers, 1983), pp. 21–24.

18. For discussions of the Chicago School see Bernard E. Meland, "Introduction: The Empirical Tradition in Theology at Chicago," *The Future of Empirical Theology* (Chicago: The University of Chicago Press, 1969); Harvey Arnold, *Near the Edge of the Battle: 1866-1960* (Chicago: The Divinity School Association of the University of Chicago, 1966); William J. Hynes, *Shirley Jackson Case and The Chicago School: The Socio-Historical Method* (Chico, California: Scholars Press, 1981); Larry E. Axel, "Process and Religion: The History of a Tradition at Chicago,"

Process Studies, VIII (Winter 1978), pp. 231–239.

19. Meland, "Introduction," p. 9.

20. Ibid.

21. Ralph Waldo Emerson, "Nature," *The Complete Essays and Other Writings of Ralph Waldo Emerson* (New York: Modern Library, 1950), p. 13.

22. Ibid., p. 33.

23. Ibid., p. 35.

24. Ibid., p. 36.

25. John E. Smith, "Introduction," Josiah Royce, *The Problem of Christianity* (Chicago: The University of Chicago Press, 1968), p. 1.

26. Josiah Royce, *The Spirit of Modern Philosophy* (Boston and New York: Houghton Mifflin Company, 1892), p. 361.

27. Bruce Kuklick, *The Rise of American Philosophy: Cambridge, Massachusetts, 1860–1920* (New Haven: Yale University Press, 1977), p. 140.

28. For example, Kuklick interprets James as an idealist. See Ibid., p. 171.

29. Joseph Haroutunian, "Theology and the American Experience," *Criterion* (Chicago), 3 (Winter 1964), 8.

30. See, e.g., Harold Bloom et al, *Deconstructionism and Criticism* (New York: The Seabury Press, 1979); Christopher Norris, *Deconstructionism: Theory and Practice* (New York: Methuen, 1982).

31. Frank Lentricchia, *After the New Criticism* (Chicago: The University of Chicago Press, 1980); Frank Lentricchia, *Criticism and Social Change* (Chicago: The University of Chicago Press, 1983).

32. Charles Altieri, "From Symbolist Thought to Immanence: The Ground of Post-Modern American Poetics," *Boundary 2*, 1 (Spring 1973), 605–641. See also G. Douglas Atkins, "Dehellenizing Literary Criticism," *College English*, 41 (March 1980), 769–779.

33. Ekbert Faas, *Towards a New American Poetics* (Santa Barbara: Scarecrow Press, 1979).

34. See especially, Jacques Derrida, *Of Grammatology*, translated by Gayatri Chakravorty Spivak (Baltimore: The Johns Hopkins University Press, 1976); Jacques Derrida, "Structure, Sign, and Play in the Discourse of the Human Sciences," *Writing and Difference*, translated

by Alan Bass (Chicago: The University of Chicago Press, 1978), pp. 278–293.

35. Richard Rorty, *Philosophy and the Mirror of Nature* (Princeton: Princeton University Press, 1979); Richard Rorty, *Consequences of Pragmatism* (Minneapolis: University of Minnesota Press, 1982).

36. Cornel West, "Nietzsche's Prefiguration of Post-Modern American Philosophy," *Boundary 2*, 9 and 10 (Spring/Fall 1981), 242.

37. Nelson Goodman, "Notes on the Well-Made World," *Partisan Review*, 51/2 (1984), 283.

38. Ibid., p. 282. See my discussion of Wheeler in Chapter 2 below.

39. Nelson Goodman, *Ways of Worldmaking* (Indianapolis: Hackett Publishing Co., 1978).

40. Daniel Bell, "The Turn to Interpretation: An Introduction," *Partisan Review*, 51/2 (1984), 217.

41. Rorty, "Dewey's Metaphysics," *Consequences*, p. 76.

42. Rorty, "Introduction," *Consequences*, p. xviii.

Chapter 1. An Empirical Interpretation: An American Theology

1. See the distinction between idealism and empiricism, set forth above in the "Introduction,"

2. Jonathan Edwards, *Religious Affections*, ed. by John E. Smith (New Haven: Yale University Press, 1969) in Jonathan Edwards, *The Works of Jonathan Edwards*, ed. by Perry Miller (6 vols.: New Haven: Yale University Press, 1966–80), II. pp. 260–265.

3. William James, "The Will to Believe," in *The Will to Believe and Other Essays on Popular Philosophy* (New York: Dover Publications, Inc., 1956), p. 18.

4. Morton White, *Science and Sentiment in America: Philosophical Thought from Jonathan Edwards to John Dewey* (New York: Oxford University Press, 1972), pp. 29, 49.

5. John Locke, *An Essay Concerning Human Understanding*, ed. by A.D. Woozley (New York: New American Library, 1974), p. 100.

6. Jonathan Edwards, "A Divine and Supernatural Light," in *Jonathan Edwards: Basic Writings*, ed. by Ola Elizabeth Winslow (New York:

New American Library, 1978), p. 129. See also Roland Andre Delat-tre's systematic study of the aesthetic dimension in Edwards's thought in *Beauty and Sensibility in the Thought of Jonathan Edwards* (New Haven: Yale University Press, 1968).

7. Edwards, *Religious Affections*, p. 96.

8. Edwards, "A Divine and Supernatural Light," p. 131; see also, Edwards, *Religious Affections*, p. 97.

9. Edwards, "A Divine and Supernatural Light," p. 130; Jonathan Edwards, "Concerning the End for Which God Created the Earth," in *Jonathan Edwards: Basic Writings*, ed. by Winslow, p. 237.

10. Jonathan Edwards, "Ideas, Sense of the Heart, Spiritual Knowledge or Conviction. Faith," in "Jonathan Edwards on the Sense of the Heart," by Perry Miller, *Harvard Theological Review*, 41/2 (April 1948), p. 137.

11. Locke, *An Essay*, pp. 306–19.

12. Edwards, "Ideas, Sense of the Heart," p. 139.

13. Ibid., p. 141; see also Jonathan Edwards, *Images or Shadows of Divine Things*, ed. by Perry Miller (New Haven: Yale University Press, 1948), p. 36.

14. Edwards, "Ideas, Sense of the Heart," p. 138.

15. Miller, "Jonathan Edwards on the Sense of the Heart," p. 124; see also Edwards, *Images*, pp. 22–24.

16. Miller, "Jonathan Edwards on the Sense of the Heart," p. 127.

17. Ibid.

18. Perry Miller, *Jonathan Edwards* (Amherst: The University of Massachusetts Press, 1981), p. 52.

19. Ibid., p. 53.

20. Norman Fiering, *Jonathan Edwards's Moral Thought and Its British Context* (Chapel Hill: The University of North Carolina Press, 1981), p. 36.

21. Ibid., p. 38.

22. Ibid., pp. 60–61. Also Vincent Tomas, in "The Modernity of Jonathan Edwards" (*New England Quarterly* 25 [March 1952], 60–84) argues, against Miller, that Edwards is a medieval rather than a modern thinker. Tomas does not speak directly to the question of epistemology, which is the crucial question here. Also William J. Wainwright, in

"Jonathan Edwards and the Language of God" (*Journal of the American Academy of Religion* 47 [December, 1980]), contends that Edwards's references to sense are intended to find in nature only "types" or "emblems" or "allegories" put in nature by God to be conceptually construed by the theologian, providing fuller knowledge of God. Much of Wainwright's case rests on the contention that "there appears no reason why Edwards should not be placed squarely within this tradition [of typological reading]" (Ibid., p. 527). In short, Wainwright's argument is undertaken by means of pursuing a possible alternative interpretation, rather than by directly criticizing Miller's own interpretation.

23. Fiering, *Jonathan Edwards*, p. 55.

24. Ibid., p. 125.

25. Ibid., pp. 55–58.

26. Ibid., pp. 124–125.

27. See also Wallace E. Anderson, Editor's Introduction to Jonathan Edwards, *Scientific and Philosophical Writings*, ed. W. E. Anderson, vol. 6 of *The Works of Jonathan Edwards* (New Haven: Yale University Press, 1980), pp. 101–103 and 111–123; Conrad Cherry, *Jonathan Edwards: A Reappraisal* (Garden City, N.Y.: Doubleday, 1966); and John F. Wilson, "Jonathan Edwards as Historian," *Church History*, 46 (1977), pp. 5–18, all of whom emphasize the Calvinistic, Augustinian and Biblical roots of Edwards's thought, sometimes against Lockean and modernist interpretations of Edwards's thought.

28. Ibid., p. 36.

29. Perry Miller, *Errand into the Wilderness* (Cambridge, Mass.: The Belknap Press of Harvard University Press, 1956), p. 180.

30. Miller, "Jonathan Edwards on the Sense of the Heart," p. 127.

31. See, e.g., David Laurence, "Jonathan Edwards, John Locke, and the Canon of Experience," *Early American Literature*, 15 (1980), pp. 107–123.

32. See John Locke, *On the Reasonableness of Christianity* (Chicago: Henry Regenry Co., no date).

33. See the discussion of deconstructionism in Chapter 2 below.

34. Miller, *Jonathan Edwards*, p. 58.

35. Fiering, *Jonathan Edwards*, p. 125.

36. Miller, "Jonathan Edwards on the Sense of the Heart," p. 125.

37. William James, *Essays in Radical Empiricism* and *A Pluralistic Universe*, 2 vols. in 1 (New York: Longmans, Green & Co., 1947), vol. 1, p. 163.

38. Ibid., p. 168.

39. Ibid., p. 150.

40. Ibid., pp. 297–300; William James, *Varieties of Religious Experience* (New York: Collier, 1976), pp. 393, 398.

41. Jonathan Edwards, "Personal Narrative," in *Jonathan Edwards: Basic Writings*, ed. by Winslow, p. 85.

42. James, *Varieties*, p. 74.

43. Alfred North Whitehead, *Process and Reality: An Essay in Cosmology*, ed. by David Ray Griffin and Donald W. Sherburne (New York: The Free Press, 1978), p. xi.

44. Alfred North Whitehead, *Modes of Thought* (New York: Macmillan, 1968), p. 151.

45. Whitehead, *Process and Reality*, p. 162.

46. Edwards, *Religious Affections*, p. 98.

47. James, *Essays in Radical Empiricism* and *A Pluralistic Universe*, vol. 1, p. 150.

48. Whtiehead, *Modes*, p. 164.

49. John Dewey, *Art as Experience*, (New York: Capricorn Books, 1958), p. 16.

50. Ibid., p. 195. This reverses, apparently, Dewey's claim in *A Common Faith* (New Haven: Yale University Press, 1952) that the "whole" of the world is "an imaginative, not a literal, idea. . . . It cannot be apprehended in knowledge nor realized in reflection" (pp. 18–19).

51. Henry Nelson Wieman, *Seeking a Faith for a New Age: Essays on the Interdependence of Religion, Science and Philosophy*, ed. by Cedric L. Hepler (Metuchen: The Scarecrow Press, Inc., 1975), pp. 52–54.

52. Robert W. Bretall, ed., *The Empirical Theology of Henry Nelson Wieman* (Carbondale and Edwardsville: Southern Illinois University Press, 1963), p. 70.

53. Ibid.

54. Henry Nelson Wieman, *The Source of Human Good* (Carbondale: Southern Illinois University Press, 1964), p. 174.

55. Ibid., p. 66.

56. Ibid., p. 67.

57. Henry Nelson Wieman, *Religious Experience and Scientific Method* (Carbondale: Southern Illinois University Press, 1971), p. 210.

58. Ibid., p. 350.

59. Ibid., p. 345.

60. Ibid., p. 343.

61. Wieman, *Seeking*, pp. 55–60; Henry Nelson Wieman and Regina Wescott-Wieman, *Normative Psychology of Religion* (Westport: Greenwood Press, 1971), pp. 186-88.

62. Bernard E. Meland, "The Root and Form of Wieman's Thought," in *The Empirical Theology of Henry Nelson Wieman*, Bretall, ed., p. 65.

63. Bernard E. Meland, *Higher Education and the Human Spirit* (Chicago: University of Chicago Press, 1953), p. 41.

64. Bernard E. Meland, *Fallible Forms and Symbols* (Philadelphia: Fortress Press, 1976), p. 24.

65. For the best expressions of Meland's epistemology see his *Faith and Culture* (New York: Oxford University Press, 1953), chapters 6, 7, and 8, and *The Realities of Faith* (New York: Oxford University Press, 1962), chapters 8 and 9. Meland's most recent book, *Fallible Forms and Symbols*, is virtually one long radically empirical critique of recent American theological presumptions (see William Dean, "Method in a Theology of Culture," *Journal of Religion* 59/4 [October, 1979], pp. 459–63).

66. Bernard E. Meland, *Higher Education*, p. 54.

67. Bernard Loomer, "The Size of God," *The American Journal of Theology and Philosophy*, forthcoming in 1987. It was originally analyzed at separate sessions, specially devoted to it, at the national meetings of the American Academy of Religion in 1978 and 1979.

68. If the "problem of evil" depends on the simultaneous retention of (1) the omnipotence of God, (2) the pure benevolence of God and (3) the existence of evil, Meland's radical empiricism has undercut the problem by eliminating the evidence for the omnipotence of God, and Loomer's radical empiricism has undercut the problem by eliminating evidence for both the omnipotence and the pure benevolence of God.

69. See especially, "Two Conceptions of Power," *Process Studies*, 6 (1976), 5–32; "The Future of Process Philosophy," in *Process Philosophy: Basic Writings*, edited by Jack R. Sibley and Pete A. Y. Gunter, pp. 513–538. For a review of Loomer's writings and lectures anticipating "The Size of God" see William Dean, "Introduction: From Integrity to Size," *The American Journal of Theology and Philosophy*, forthcoming in 1986.

70. Loomer, "The Size of God," p. 6 of the original paper.

71. Ibid., pp. 42–45.

72. *Philosophers Speak of God*, ed. by Charles Hartshorne and William L. Reese (Chicago: University of Chicago Press, 1953), p. 3.

73. Bernard Meland has said, "The process mode of thought derived from Whitehead's writing tends to revert to an all-out commitment to coherence as the underlying and ultimate principle of giving meaning to existence. When this occurs, process thought takes on rational overtones reminiscent of Hegelianism, against which the radical empiricism of James and Bergson protested so vehemently" (Meland, *Fallible Forms*, p. 110). This tendency is illustrated even in rationalistic process theology's critiques of empirical process theology (see, e.g., Charles Hartshorne's argument that Wieman's doctrine of God is incomplete because it fails to use analogical reasoning to derive a notion of how God is a person with the capacities of a person [Hartshorne and Reese, eds., *Philosophers*, pp. 404–08]). Hartshorne appears oblivious to Wieman's empiricist reasons for rejecting analogical reasoning and for accepting the incompleteness which that rejection causes. For a more complete discussion of the distinction between Hartshorne's and Whitehead's rationalism, a question only tangential to this chapter, see the chapters by David Griffin and Lewis Ford, especially pages 47ff. and 68ff. in *Two Process Philosophers*, ed. by Lewis Ford (Tallahassee, Florida: American Academy of Religion, 1973).

74. Charles Hartshorne, *A Natural Theology for Our Time* (LaSalle, Illinois: Open Court Publishing Co., 1967), p. 133.

75. Schubert M. Ogden, "Present Prospects for Empirical Theology," in *The Future of Empirical Theology*, ed. by Bernard E. Meland (Chicago: The University of Chicago Press, 1969), pp. 76–88.

76. Schubert M. Ogden, *The Reality of God and Other Essays* (New York: Harper and Row, 1966), p. 36.

77. Ibid., pp. 43, 48.

78. Meland, *Fallible Forms*, pp. xiv, 121.

79. Bernard E. Meland, "Can Empirical Theology Learn Something from Phenomenology?" in *The Future of Empirical Theology*, ed. by Meland, p. 297.

Chapter 2. An Historicist Interpretation: The Deconstruction and Reconstruction of Religious Knowledge

1. Bernard M. Loomer, "The Future of Process Philosophy," in *Process Philosophy: Basic Writings*, ed. Jack R. Sibley and Pete A. Y. Gunter (Washington, D.C.: University Press of America, 1978), p. 531.

2. Paul de Man, *Blindness and Insight: Essays in the Rhetoric of Contemporary Criticism* (New York: Oxford University Press, 1971), p. 110.

3. Jacques Derrida, *Of Grammatology*, trans. Gayatri Charkavorty Spivak (Baltimore and London: Johns Hopkins University Press, 1976), pp. 7–15.

4. Jacques Derrida, "Structure, Sign, and Play in the Discourse of the Human Sciences," *Writing and Difference*, trans. Alan Bass (Chicago: University of Chicago Press, 1978), p. 291.

5. Derrida, *Of Grammatology*, p. 9.

6. Ibid., p. 163.

7. Ibid., p. 159.

8. Ibid., p. 47.

9. Ibid., p. 163.

10. Ibid., p. 324.

11. Jacques Derrida, "Difference," in *Speech and Phenomena and Other Essays on Husserl's Theory of Signs*, trans. David B. Allison (Evanston, Ill.: Northwestern University Press, 1973), p. 145.

12. Derrida, *Of Grammatology*, p. 158.

13. Ibid., p. 70; phrase bracketed in the text.

14. Ibid., p. 158.

15. *The New York Review of Books* is a natural vehicle for such

purposes. See Dennis Donoghue, "Deconstructing Deconstructionism," (a review of *Deconstruction and Criticism*, by Harold Bloom, Paul de Man, Jacques Derrida, Geoffrey H. Hartman, and J. Hillis Miller), 27 (June 12, 1980); John R. Searle, "The World Turned Upside Down," (a review of *On Deconstruction: Theory and Criticism after Structuralism*, by Jonathan Culler), 30 (October 27, 1983).

16. M. H. Abrams, "The Deconstructive Angel," *Critical Inquiry* 3 (Spring 1977), 429.

17. E. D. Hirsch, Jr., *The Aims of Interpretation* (Chicago: The University of Chicago Press, 1976), p. 147.

18. Frank Lentricchia, *After the New Criticism* (Chicago: The University of Chicago Press, 1980), p. 262.

19. Rene Descartes, *Meditations on First Philosophy*, trans. by Laurence J. Lafleur (Indianapolis: The Bobbs-Merrill Co., 1960), p. 26.

20. Lentricchia, *After the New Criticism*, p. 175.

21. Ibid., p. 177.

22. Ibid.

23. Ibid., p. 262.

24. Ibid., p. 159.

25. There are, of course, more moderate interpretations of deconstructionism among students of literature. G. Douglas Atkins, for example, has not only accomplished this, but has effectively suggested positive theological implications of deconstructionism. (See G. Douglas Atkins, "Dehellenizing Literary Criticism," *College English* 41 (March 1980): 769–779.)

26. Thomas J. J. Altizer et al., *Deconstruction and Theology* (New York: Crossroad Publishing Co., 1982); Mark C. Taylor, *Deconstructing Theology* (New York, NY and Chico, CA: Crossroad Publishing Co. and Scholars Press, 1982); Mark C. Taylor, *Erring: A Postmodern A/theology* (Chicago: The University of Chicago Press, 1984).

27. Ibid., p. 53.

28. Ibid., p. viii.

29. Alfred North Whitehead, *Process and Reality: An Essay in Cosmology*, Corrected Edition, edited by David Ray Griffin and Donald W. Sherburne (New York: The Free Press, 1978), p. 21.

30. Ibid., p. 22.

31. For an elaboration of the centrality of the notion of experience in Whitehead and James, see my "Radical Empiricism and Religious Art," *Journal of Religion* 21 (April 1981), 168–87.

32. John Archibald Wheeler, "Beyond the Black Hole," in *Some Strangeness in Proportion: A Centennial Symposium to Celebrate the Achievements of Albert Einstein*, ed. Harry Woolf (Reading, Mass.: Addison-Wesley Publishing Co., 1980), p. 350.

33. Ibid. The second uses of "before" and "after" refer to the first phases of the big bang and the last phases of gravitational collapse; the first uses of "before" and "after" indicate that beyond those phases there is not time, and that time is not an ultimate category in the description of nature, (Ibid., p. 372).

34. Ibid., p. 363. Wheeler has provided, I believe, a way through the middle of the dilemma of relativism and absolutism, or shown that that dilemma commits the fallacy of the excluded middle. In effect, one need not choose between paying the price of relativism to get relationality and paying the price of absolutism to get order; a middle option is possible. In a participatory universe, relationality exists in the observer-observed interaction, and order exists in the temporary life of laws.

35. Freeman Dyson, "Comment on the Topic 'Beyond the Black Hole,' " in Ibid., 376-377. See also J. A. Wheeler, "Genesis and Observership," in *Foundational Problems in the Special Sciences*, ed. R.E. Butts and J. Hintikka (Dordrecht and Boston: D. Reidel Publishing Co., 1977), pp. 3–33; Richard Schlegel, *Superposition and Interaction Coherence in Physics* (Chicago: University of Chicago Press, 1980), chap. 10.

36. Alfred North Whitehead, *Modes of Thought* (New York: Capricorn Books, 1958), p. 154.

37. Ibid., pp. 154–155.

38. Ibid., p. 93.

39. Ibid., p. 92.

40. Ibid., p. 155.

41. Ibid., p. 154.

42. Ibid., p. 93.

43. See esp. William James, *Essays in Radical Empiricism and A Pluralistic Universe*, 2 vols. in 1 (New York: Longmans, Green & Co., 1947), vol. 1, chap. 4; John Dewey, *Experience and Nature* (New York: Dover Publications, 1958), chap. 1.

44. William James, "Is Life Worth Living?" *The Will to Believe and Other Essays in Popular Philosophy and Human Immortality: Two Supposed Objections to the Doctrine* (New York: Dover Publications, 1956), p. 60.

45. John Dewey, *A Common Faith* (New Haven: Yale University Press, 1934), pp. 14–19.

46. Whitehead, *Process and Reality*, pp. 40, 96, 116.

47. Derrida, *Of Grammatology*, p. 14.

48. Ibid., p. 15.

49. Derrida's pragmatism can be seen, for example, in his "Difference," p. 141; and in eds. Richard Macksey and Eugene Donato, *The Structuralist Controversy* (Baltimore: Johns Hopkins Press, 1972), where Derrida says, "I believe that the center is a function, not a being—a reality, but a function." (p. 271).

50. See, e.g., Ilya Prigogine, *From Being to Becoming: Time and Complexity in the Physical Sciences* (San Francisco: W. H. Freeman & Co., 1980).

51. See, e.g., Gustaf Wingren, *Flight from Creation* (Minneapolis: Augsburg Publishing House, 1971).

52. Whitehead, *Process and Reality*, pp. 110–112.

53. James, "The Will to Believe," p. 52.

54. James, "Is Life Worth Living?" p. 61.

55. Ibid.

56. See Chapter III below.

57. If the question of the morality of God turns in part on empirical evidence of types of natural activities, then an essay such as Steven Jay Gould's discussion of the predation of wasp larvae ("Nonmoral Nature," *Natural History*, vol. 91 [February 1982]) could be seen as providing powerful evidence for the nonmorality of God.

58. I have outlined an aesthetic ethic for process theology in *Love Before the Fall* (Philadelphia: Westminster Press, 1976).

59. See Alfred North Whitehead, *The Function of Reason* (Boston: Beacon Press, 1950), p. 7.

60. See Whitehead, *Modes of Thought*, p. 120.

61. Robert B. Laurin, "Tradition and Canon," in *Tradition and*

Theology in the Old Testament, ed. Douglas Knight (Philadelphia: Fortress Press, 1977), p. 267.

62. Henry Nelson Wieman, *The Source of Human Good* (Carbondale: Southern Illinois University Press, 1964), p. 56.

63. Bernard E. Meland, *Fallible Forms and Symbols* (Philadelphia: Fortress Press, 1976), p. 151.

64. Bernard M. Loomer, "The Size of God," *The American Journal of Theology and Philosophy*, forthcoming in 1987. The reference is to pages 63-65 of the original paper, which was analyzed at separate sessions, specially devoted to it, at national meetings of the American Academy of Religion in 1978 and 1979.

65. Derrida, "Structure, Sign, and Play," pp. 279-280.

66. Derrida, *Of Grammatology*, p. 12.

67. M. H. Abrams, "The Deconstructive Angel," p. 431.

68. M. H. Abrams, "How to Do Things with Texts," *Partisan Review*, 46 (1979), p. 573.

69. Wayne C. Booth, " 'Preserving the Exemplar': or, How Not to Dig Our Own Graves," *Critical Inquiry*, 3 (Spring 1977), pp. 407-423.

Chapter 3. A Pragmatic Interpretation: The Tragedy of the Liberals

1. William James, "Is Life Worth Living?" *The Will to Believe and Other Essays in Popular Philosophy; Human Immortality: Two Supposed Objections to the Doctrine* (New York: Dover Publications, Inc., 1956), 1, p. 37.

2. Sydney E. Ahlstrom, *A Religious History of the American People* (New Haven: Yale University Press, 1972), p. 784. He quotes from H. Richard Niebuhr, *The Kingdom of God in America* (New York: Harper and Row, 1959), p. 193.

3. James, "Is Life Worth Living?" p. 38.

4. Shailer Mathews, *New Faith for Old: An Autobiography* (New York: The Macmillan Co., 1936), p. 126.

5. Mathews, *New Faith for Old*, p. 131.

6. Reinhold Niebuhr, *An Interpretation of Christian Ethics* (New

York: Harper and Brothers, 1935), pp. 173, 177.

7. Reinhold Niebuhr, *The Nature and Destiny of Man: A Christian Interpretation* (New York: Charles Scribner's Sons, 1949), 1, p. 104.

8. Ibid., p. 14.

9. James, "Is Life Worth Living?" p. 61.

10. William James, *Pragmatism*, in *Pragmatism and Four Essays from the Meaning of Truth* (Cleveland and New York: The World Publishing Co., 1964), p. 190.

11. Ibid., pp. 190–191.

12. Sydney Hook, "Pragmatism and the Tragic Sense of Life," *Contemporary American Philosophy*, Second Series, edited by John E. Smith (New York: Humanities Press, Inc., 1970), pp. 170–193.

13. Shirley Jackson Case, *The Christian Philosophy of History* (Chicago: The University of Chicago Press, 1943), p. 175.

14. Ibid., p. 172.

15. See Charles Morris, *The Pragmatic Movement in American Philosophy* (New York: George Braziller, 1970), pp. 174–191.

16. William Jones, *Essays in Radical Empiricism: A Pluralistic Universe*, 2 vols. in 1 (New York: Longmans, Green and Co., 1947), 1, pp. 44ff.

17. John Dewey, *Art as Experience* (New York: Capricorn Books, 1958), pp. 192–193.

18. Case, *The Christian Philosophy of History*, p. 193; see also William J. Hynes, *Shirley Jackson Case and the Chicago School* (Chico, California: Scholars Press, 1981), p. 71.

19. Shirley Jackson Case, *The Origin of Christian Supernaturalism* (Chicago: The University of Chicago Press, 1946), pp. 232–234.

20. "Great Men and Their Environment," *The Will to Believe*, pp. 225-226.

21. James, "Great Men," p. 227.

22. William James, *Pragmatism*, p. 147. See also Philip P. Wiener, *Evolution and the Founders of Pragmatism* (Cambridge: Harvard University Press, 1949), p. 104; and Lewis R. Rambo, "Evolution, Community, and the Strenuous Life: The Context of William James' *Varieties of Religious Experience*," *Encounter: Creative Theological Scholarship*, 43 (Summer 1982), esp. 240-242.

23. William James, *The Varieties of Religious Experience* (New York: Macmillan Publishing Co., 1981), p. 31.

24. Ibid., pp. 127ff.

25. Ibid., p. 391.

26. Ibid., p. 393.

27. Ibid., p. 31.

28. James, *Pragmatism*, p. 60.

29. Richard Rorty, *Consequences of Pragmatism (Essays, 1972–1980)* (Minneapolis: University of Minnesota Press, 1982), p. 150.

30. Richard Rorty, *Philosophy and the Mirror of Nature* (Princeton, New Jersey: Princeton University Press, 1982), pp. 9, 13.

31. Ibid., pp. 389–94.

32. Rorty, *Consequences of Pragmatism*, pp. xiii-xlvii, 52.

33. Ibid., p. xlii.

34. Ibid.

35. Rorty introduces the image of the conversation "as the ultimate context within which knowledge is to be understood" in, Rorty, *Philosophy and the Mirror of Nature*, pp. 389ff.

36. Cornel West, book review of Rorty, *Philosophy and the Mirror of Nature* in *Union Seminary Quarterly Review*, 37 (Fall/Winter 1981), p. 184.

37. Ibid.

38. Cornel West, "Nietzsche's Prefiguration of Postmodern American Philosophy," *Boundary 2*, 9 and 10 (Spring/Fall 1981), 265.

39. Cornel West, *Prophesy Deliverance! An Afro-American Revolutionary Christianity* (Philadelphia: The Westminster Press, 1982).

40. Mark Lilla, "On Goodman, Putnam, and Rorty: The Return of the 'Given.' " *Partisan Review*, 51/2 (1984), 233.

41. Kenneth Burke, "William Carlos Williams, 1883-1963," *Language as Symbolic Action: Essays on Life, Literature, and Method* (Berkeley and Los Angeles: University of California Press, 1966), pp. 282-293.

42. Frank Lentricchia, *Criticism and Social Change* (Chicago: The University of Chicago Press, 1983).

43. James, "Is Life Worth Living?" p. 52.

44. Richard Bernstein, *Beyond Objectivism and Relativism: Science, Hermeneutics, and Praxis* (Philadelphia: University of Pennsylvania Press, 1983).

45. Jeffrey Stout, *The Flight from Authority: Religion, Morality, and the Quest for Autonomy* (Notre Dame: University of Notre Dame Press, 1981), p. xi.

46. William A. Clebsch, *American Religious Thought: A History* (Chicago: The University of Chicago Press, 1973), p. xvi.

47. Henry S. Levinson, "Santayana's Contribution to American Religious Philosophy," *Journal of the American Academy of Religion*, 52 (March 1984), 49.

48. Hynes, *Shirley Jackson Case*, p. 119.

49. Mathews, *New Faith for Old*, p. 70.

50. Bernard Eugene Meland, *Faith and Culture* (New York: Oxford University Press, 1953), p. 170. See also William D. Dean, "Fireflies in a Quagmire," *Journal of Religion* (October 1968), which discusses the sense of evil in recent liberal theology.

51. Bernard M. Loomer, "The Size of God," *The American Journal of Theology and Philosophy*, forthcoming in 1987.

Chapter 4. An Aesthetic Interpretation: The Elusive "It"

1. Alfred North Whitehead, *Adventures of Ideas* (New York: The Free Press, 1967), p. 262.

2. Ibid., p. 269.

3. Whitehead, *Religion in the Making* (New York: The Macmillan Co., 1954), p. 138.

4. Whitehead, *Adventures of Ideas*, p. 265.

5. Whitehead, *Religion in the Making*, p. 138.

6. Sherburne's influence is most pronounced in biblical interpretation in the work of William A. Beardslee; see, for example, *A House for Hope* (Philadelphia: Westminster Press, 1972), Ch. 8. While a group of scholars does generate its own voice, it appears, nevertheless, that Sherburne has influenced the group of biblical scholars who have written very effectively in a "thematic issue" of the *Journal of the American Academy of Religion*, entitled "New Testament Interpretation from

a Process Perspective" (Vol. 47, March, 1979). The issue includes articles by John B. Cobb, Jr., William Beardslee, David Lull, Russell Pregeant, Theodore J. Weeden, Sr., and Barry A. Woodbridge. Beardslee sets the tone of the issue when he speaks of "reading of a text through a theory of propositions" (p. 35, see also p. 65); and Woodbridge summarizes the group's contention "that a text is a configuration of various linguistic symbols which tend to elicit 'lures for feeling' technically called 'propositional feelings' . . ." (pp. 122-23). For a comment on propositional notions of Christology see John Cobb, Jr., *Christ in a Pluralistic Age* (Philadelphia: Westminster Press, 1975), pp. 14-15, and of sacramentology see Bernard J. Lee, S. M., "The Sacrament of Creative Transformation," *Process Studies*, 8, (Winter 1978), 240-52.

7. See Donald Sherburne, "Meaning and Music," *The Journal of Aesthetics and Art Criticism*, 24, (Summer 1966), 579-83.

8. Alfred North Whitehead, *Process and Reality: An Essay in Cosmology*, Corrected Edition edited by David Ray Griffin and Donald W. Sherburne (London and New York: The Free Press, 1978), pp. 280, 111; Charles Hartshorne *Man's Vision of God and the Logic of Theism* (Hamden, Connecticut: Archon Books, 1964), p. 212.

9. This is not to identify Sherburne with the skeptical mind-body dualism established by Descartes, but is to suggest that Sherburne's type of analysis invests primary confidence in an intellectual construct, the propositional feeling, and proceeds to examine the world on the basis of that construct, all in a way somewhat reminiscent of Descartes.

10. Donald W. Sherburne, *A Whiteheadian Aesthetic: Some Implications of Whitehead's Metaphysical Speculation* (New Haven: Yale University Press, 1961), p. 171.

11. Ibid., p. 155.

12. Ibid., p. 179.

13. Ibid., pp. 10-11.

14. See E. D. Hirsch, Jr., *The Aims of Interpretation* (Chicago: The University of Chicago Press, 1976), Chapters 1-5, especially his attacks on "perspectivism."

15. Whitehead, *Process and Reality*, Part II, Chapter 8; Alfred North Whitehead, *Symbolism: Its Meaning and Effect* (New York: Capricorn Books, 1959), Ch. 2.

16. Ibid., pp. 56-57.

17. Ibid.

18. Alfred North Whitehead, *Modes of Thought* (New York: The Free Press, 1966), p. 119.

19. Ibid., pp. 120-21.

20. Such an aesthetic would concentrate, for example, on what John Cobb, following Vernon Lee, calls the "hearer" of music—that is, one who reacts to music as it is felt in the mode of causal efficacy. It would depart, obviously, from Cobb's contention that "listeners," responding in the mode of presentational immediacy, are alone "capable of useful criticism or indeed of any serious discussion of musical composition" (John B. Cobb, Jr., "Toward Clarity in Aesthetics," *Philosophy and Phenomenological Research*, 18 [1957], 178).

21. Whitehead, *Modes of Thought*, p. 116.

22. Ibid., p. 4.

23. *The Autobiography of William Carlos Williams* (New York: Random House, 1951), pp. 288-89.

24. *The Collected Earlier Poems of William Carlos Williams* (Norfolk, Conn.: New Directions Books, 1951), p. 277.

25. See J. Hillis Miller, "Introduction," *William Carlos Williams: A Collection of Critical Essays*, ed. J. Hillis Miller (Englewood Cliffs: Prentice-Hall, 1966).

26. John Dewey, *Art as Experience* (New York, N.Y.: Capricorn Books, 1958), pp. 14-15.

27. Ibid., p. 16; see also pp. 65-75.

28. Ibid., pp. 191-95; see also John Dewey, *Experience and Nature* (New York, N.Y.: Dover Publications, 1958), p. xii.

29. Dewey, *Art as Experience*, pp. 37ff.

30. See William Shea's effort to establish this and to show the religious meaning manifest for Dewey through the aesthetic discernment of quality in "Qualitative Wholes: Aesthetic and Religious Experience in the Work of John Dewey," *The Journal of Religion*, 60, (January 1980), 32-50.

31. Whitehead, *Symbolism*, pp. 52, 38, 39; see also *Modes of Thought*, Chs. 6 and 8.

32. Whitehead, *Adventures of Ideas*, p. 262.

33. William James, *Essays in Radical Empiricism, A Pluralistic Uni-*

verse, 2 vols. in 1 (New York: Longmans, Green and Company, 1947), 1, p. 23.

34. Dewey, *Art as Experience*, pp. 35–37; italics are Dewey's.

35. Bergson, *Creative Evolution* (Westport: Greenwood Press, 1975), pp. 191–95.

36. Whitehead, *Modes of Thought*, p. 113.

37. Ibid., p. 117.

38. William James, *The Varieties of Religious Experience* (New York: Collier Books, 1976), p. 31.

Chapter 5. *A Formal Interpretation: The Fate of an American Theology*

1. George Santayana, "The Genteel Tradition in American Philosophy," *Winds of Doctrine* (New York: Charles Scribner's Sons, 1913), p. 203.

2. Donald H. Meyer, "Secular Transcendence: The American Religious Humanists," *American Quarterly*, 34 (Winter 1982), 34.

3. Sydney E. Ahlstrom, *A Religious History of the American People* (New Haven and London: Yale University Press, 1972), p. 634.

4. William Carlos Williams, *The Autobiography of William Carlos Williams* (New York: Random House, 1951), p. 146.

5. Ibid.

6. William Carlos Williams, *The Embodiment of Knowledge* (New York: New Directions Books, 1974), p. 52.

7. William Carlos Williams, *Selected Essays of William Carlos Williams* (New York: Random House, 1954), pp. 33–34.

8. Williams, *Embodiment*, p. 48.

9. Ibid., pp. 49, 53.

10. Margaret Glynne Lloyd, *William Carlos Williams's Paterson: A Critical Reappraisal* (Rutherford, Madison, Teaneck: Farleigh Dickenson University Press, 1980), p. 34.

11. Alfred North Whitehead, *Symbolism: Its Meaning and Effect* (New York: Capricorn Books, 1959), p. 57.

12. Robert von Hallberg, *Charles Olson: The Scholar's Art* (Cam-

bridge, Mass.: Harvard University Press, 1978), p. 82.

13. Ibid., p. 82.

14. Lloyd, *William Carlos Williams*, p. 191.

15. Whitehead, *Religion in the Making* (New York: New American Library, 1974), p. 39.

16. Ibid., p. 141.

17. Alfred North Whitehead, *Science and the Modern World* (New York: Macmillan, 1962), p. 85.

18. Alfred North Whitehead, *Modes of Thought* (New York: Macmillan, 1968), p. 174. See Frank Burch Brown's excellent discussion of Whitehead's implicit notion of the connection between theology and poetry. ("Poetry and the Possibility of Theology: Whitehead's Views Reconsidered," *Journal of the American Academy of Religion*, 50 (December 1982), 507-20.

19. Randall Jarell, "Introduction," *Selected Poems of William Carlos Williams* (New York: New Directions Books, 1969), p. xi.

20. J. Hillis Miller, "Introduction," *William Carlos Williams: A Collection of Critical Essays*, ed. by J. Hillis Miller, (Englewood Cliffs, N.J.: Prentice-Hall, 1966), p. 6.

21. Ekbert Faas, *Towards a New American Poetics: Essays and Interviews* (Santa Barbara: Black Sparrow Press, 1979), p. 14.

22. William J. Hynes, *Shirley Jackson Case and the Chicago School* (Chico, CA: Scholars Press, 1981), p. x.

23. *Process Philosophy and Social Thought*, ed. by John B. Cobb, Jr. and W. Widick Schroeder (Chicago: Center for the Scientific Study of Religion, 1981).

24. See especially, Cornel West, "Nietzsche's Prefiguration of Postmodern American Philosophy," *Boundary 2*, 9 and 10 (Spring/Fall 1981), 241-269; Cornel West, book review of Richard Rorty, *Philosophy and the Mirror of Nature* in *Union Seminary Quarterly Review*, 37 (Fall/Winter 1981-1982), 179-185; Cornel West, *Prophesy Deliverance! An Afro-American Revolutionary Christianity* (Philadelphia: Westminster Press, 1982).

25. Robert W. Funk, "The Watershed of the American Biblical Tradition: The Chicago School, First Phase, 1892-1920," *Journal of Biblical Literature*, 95 (March 1976), 9.

26. Ibid., p. 19.

27. Ibid., p. 7. Work by Leander Keck, indicates that at least the influence of the Chicago School in biblical studies has not been totally eclipsed, as Funk suggests. See Leander Keck, "On the Ethos of Early Christians," *Journal of the American Academy of Religion*, 47 (September 1974), 435–52; Wayne Meeks, *The First Urban Christians* (New Haven: Yale University Press, 1983); Norman Gottwald, *The Tribes of Yahweh: A Sociology of Religion of Liberated Israel*, 1250–1050 B.C.E. (Mary Knoll, New York: Orbis Books, 1979).

28. Williams, *Autobiography*, p. 391.

29. Lloyd, *William Carlos Williams*, p. 179.

30. Williams, *Essays*, p. 157.

31. Williams, *The Selected Letters of William Carlos Williams*, ed. by John C. Thirwall (New York: McDowell, Obolensky, 1957), p. 224.

32. John C. Thirwall, "William Carlos Williams as Correspondent," *The Literary Review*, 1 (Autumn 1957), p. 18; William Carlos Williams, *In the American Grain* (New York: New Directions Books, 1956), p. 109.

33. William Carlos Williams, *Paterson* (New York: New Directions Books, 1963), p. 3.

34. Williams, *Embodiment*, p. 12.

35. Paul Mariani, *William Carlos Williams: A New World Naked* (New York: McGraw-Hill, 1981), p. 497.

36. Williams, *Paterson*, p. 81.

37. Ibid., p. 144.

38. Ibid., p. 176.

39. Ibid., p. 178.

40. Ibid., p. 40.

41. Charles Olson, *Selected Writings of Charles Olson*, ed. by Robert Greeley (New York: New Directions, 1976), pp. 16–17; Olson's capitalizations.

42. Donald M. Kartiganer, "Process and Product: A Study of Modern Literary Form," *The Massachusetts Review*, 12 (Spring 1971), 306.

43. Ibid., p. 301; Henri Bergson, *Introduction to Metaphysics*, translated by T. E. Hulme (New York: no publisher listed, 1912), p. 21.

44. Kartiganer, "Process," p. 297.

45. John B. Cobb, Jr., "Forward" to Marjorie Hewitt Suchocki, *God-Christ-Church* (New York: Crossroad, 1982), p. vii.

46. "The Holocaust and Theology," a written but unpublished lecture delivered in 1975.

47. Gerhard von Rad, *The Problem of the Hexateuch and Other Essays* (New York: McGraw-Hill Book Company, 1955).

48. Gerhard von Rad, *Old Testament Theology* (2 vols.; New York: Harper and Brothers, 1962), Vol. 1, especially the "Preface."

Index

Abrams, M.H., 65; on Derrida, 45
Adam, Karl, 102
Adventures of Ideas, 97
Aestheticism, 77-79, 81
Aesthetics: Dewey's, 96-98;
  Emerson's, 84; and hedonism,
  78; of music, 138 n.20; of radical
  empiricism, 29-31; Whitehead's,
  87-99
After the New Criticism, 46, 81
Ahlstrom, Sydney, IX; *A Religious
  History of the American People*, 67;
  Theology in America, IX
The Aims of Interpretation, 46
Altizer, Thomas, 48, 50
*American Journal of Theology and
  Philosophy*, 107
American empirical theology:
  historicism not applied in, 36-39;
  role of interpreting historian in,
  114-118; new form for, 112-118
American religious empiricism: and
  construction, 41-42

deconstruction applied to, 55-63;
  distinguished from German
  liberalism, 6-7; and history, X;
  and liberalism, 5-12; and post-
  modernism, 12-17; pragmatism
  and the tragic sense in, 69-85;
  rejection of positivism by, 20;
  and science, X; student of, as
  interpreting historian, 118;
  theological form of questioned,
  101-102; tragic sense in, 67-85;
  and value, 77-85; and W.C.
  Williams, 105
American Religious Thought, 84
Ames, Edward Scribner, 9, 73, 84
anti-deconstructionism, 45-46
Art As Experience, 29-31, 96-98
Atkins, G. Douglas, 130 n.25
Ayer, A.J., 14

Barth, Karl, 56, 102-103, 108; *The
  Epistle to the Romans*, 102

143

Becker, Carl, *Every Man His Own Historian*, 115
Bell, Daniel, 16
Bergson, Henri, 98; and cognition, 90-91; *Creative Evolution*, 30; on reality, 113
Bernhardt, William Henry, XI, 10
Bernstein, Richard, *Beyond Objectivism and Relativism*, 16, 82
Bible: Hebrew, 2-5, 116; New Testament, 116
The Bible and Liberation: Political and Social Hermeneutics, 5, 117
biblical criticism, 107-108
Booth, Wayne, 65
Boston Personalists, 7
Brauer, Jerald, XII
Briggs, Charles A., 9
British empirical Enlightenment, 8-9, 19
Brown, William Adams, 7
Browning, Don, XII
Burton, Ernest Dewitt, 9, 107
Burke, Kenneth, and the writer's social obligations, 81
Bushnell, Horace, 7

Case, Shirley Jackson, X, 9, 68, 117; biblical scholarship and, 107-108; and empirical aesthetics, 99; and pragmatism, 72-77; and process theology, 38; radical empiricism implicit in work of, 30; on the religious community, 84
Chicago School of Theology, IX-XII; and American religious empiricism, 9-10; biblical scholarship and, 107-108; deconstructionist historicism and, 58; and empirical aesthetics, 99; and liberation theology, 117; and optimism, 67-69; and pragmatism, 84-85; and process theology, 38; and radical empiricism, 30

Clarke, William Newton, 7
Clebsch, William, *American Religious Thought*, 84
Cobb, John, Jr., 34, 114; on musical aesthetics, 138 n.20
A Common Faith, 31
Comte, Auguste, 14
Consequences of Pragmatism, 16, 78
cosmology, of American empiricism, 49
Creative Evolution, 30
Critical Inquiry, 65
Criticism and Social Change, 81, 115
Croce, Benedetto, 90

Darwin, Charles: *The Origin of the Species*, 75; and the tragic sense, 70-71
Darwinism, 9
Deconstruction and Theology, 48, 50
Deconstructing Theology, 48
Deconstructionism, X; applied to American religious empiricism, 55-63; generalization and, 63-66; moderate interpretations of, 130 n.25; and science, 51-55; and social history, 42-51; in theology, 48
de Man, Paul, 15, 47; criticised by Lentricchia, 81; on Derrida, 43
Descartes, René: his intellectualism rejected, 21; *Meditations*, 21
Dewey, John, 41; aesthetics of, 29-31, 96-97; and American religious empiricism, IX; *Art as Experience*, 29, 96, 98; and cognition, 90-91; *A Common Faith*, 31; *Experience and Nature*, 29; and historicism, 48-50; and objective value, 83-84; and post-modernism, 16-17; and radical empiricism, 29-32; and scientific historicism, 54-55
Derrida, Jacques, X; criticism of, 45; deconstructionism and social

history, 42-51; defended by
Lentricchia, 46-47; and historical
generalization, 63-66; historicism
and the empirical philosophers,
48-51; limits of his deconstructionism, 50; and post-modernism,
15-16; and pragmatic knowledge
of God, 57; on theological
deconstructionism, 56; and the
Yale critics, 47-48
The Divine Relativity, 35
dualism: avoided by pragmatists, 82-
83; Ed Hirsch, Jr.'s, 46;
modernism and Descartes's, 46;
of pietistic liberals, 8; Plato's, 54;
and radical empiricism, 83-84;
rejected by American empiricists,
48-49; replaced by unity, 6;
Sherburne's, 137 n.9; and W.C.
Williams, 106
Dynamics of Faith, 121, n.13
Dyson, Freeman, 53

Edwards, Jonathan, 1, 124-125 n.22;
American religious empiricism
implicit in the work of, IX; and
objective value, 83; and radical
empiricism, 20-26
Einstein, Albert, 51, 53
Eliot, T.S., *The Waste Land*,
102-103
Emerson, Ralph Waldo, 7, 10, 84
Empirical liberals, *See* Liberalism,
empirical
Empiricism: cosmology of, 49;
distinguished from idealism, 10-
11; interpretation and, 13; and
positivism, 14; seventeenth
century, 13
Enlightenment Christians, IX
The Enlightenment in America, 8
The Epistle to the Romans, 102
Erring: A Postmodern A/theology, 48
*An Essay Concerning Human
Understanding*, 22-26, 71

Essays in Radical Empiricism, 98
Every Man His Own Historian, 115
Existentialism: and interpretation,
13; and Tillich, 7
Experience and Nature, 29

Faas, Ekbert, *Towards a New
American Poetics*, 15, 107
Fiering, Norman, *Jonathan Edward's
Moral Thought and Its British
Context*, 24-26
*The First Urban Christians: The Social
World of the Apostle Paul*, 5, 116
*The Flight from Authority: Religion,
Morality and the Quest for
Autonomy*, 82
Foster, George Burman, 9, 84
Foucault, Michel, 48
The Function of Reason, 49
Fundamentalism, 69-71
Funk, Robert, 107
The Future of Empirical Theology, 10

Gager, John G; *Kingdom and
Community: An Anthropological
Approach to Civilization*, 3, 116
Gamwell, Franklin, XII
Gilkey, Langdon, XII
God: morality of, 132 n.57; and the
tropism towards complexity,
62-63
Goodman, Nelson, 80; *Ways of
Worldmaking*, 16
Gottwald, Norman: ed., *The Bible
and Liberation: Political and Social
Hermeneutics*, 5; *The Tribes of
Israel: A Sociology of the Religion
of Liberated Israel*, 5, 116
Gould, Steven Jay, 132 n.57

Haroutunian, Joseph, 12
Hartman, Geoffrey, 15, 47
Hartshorne, Charles, XI, 42, 56; *The
Divine Relativity*, 35; *Man's Vision
of God*, 34-35; *A Natural Theology*

for Our Time, 35; as a rationalistic process theologian, 34-35
Harvard Theological Review, 23,
25-26
Hedonism, 78
Hegel, Georg, 7
Hermeneutics, 16, 25
Hirsch, E.D., Jr., The Aims of
Interpretation, 46
Historicism: applied to American
religious empiricism, 55-63;
central to empirical theology, 42-
43; Cornel West on, 79-80; and
deconstructionism, 42-51;
Derrida's, 42-51; and emergence,
75-77; and the empirical
philosophers, 48-51; God-
language as a part of, 61-63; as a
literary approach in American
empirical theology, 114-118;
Meland's, 37-38; not applied in
American religious empiricism,
36-39; and pragmatism, 70;
religious, XI, XII; and science,
51-55; "thick" and "thin," 80;
and value, 77-85; and W.C.
Williams's Paterson, 109-112
A History of the Pentateuchal
Traditions, 5
Hocking, William Ernest, 11
Hook, Sydney, 66, 71
Hume, David, 8-9; and Whitehead,
105
Hutchinson, William R., The
Modernist Impulse in American
Protestantism, 120-121 n.11
Hynes, William J., Shirley Jackson
Case and the Chicago School, 107

Idealism: denied by W.C. Williams,
103-104; distinguished from
empiricism, 10-11; epistemological, 69; rejected by
Sherburne, 90-91
Iliff School of Theology, 10

Interpretation, XII, XIII; and
Derrida, 45; and post-
modernism, 14-17; tradition of
biblical, 2-5
An Interpretation of Christian Ethics,
68
"Is Life Worth Living? " 55, 67

James, William, 9, 11-12, 41; and
aesthetic value, 77-79; and
American religious empiricism,
IX; and cognition, 90-91; and an
empirical aesthetic in religion, 99;
Essays in Radical Empiricism, 98;
and historical emergence, 75-77;
and historicism, 48-50; "Is Life
Worth Living?," 55, 67; and
monism, 28; and objective value,
82-84; and optimism, 67; and
post-modernism, 17; and pragmatism, 17, 57; and radical
empiricism, 26-29; and scientific
historicism, 54-55; and the tragic
sense, 71, 73, 75-78, 82-84; and
tropism toward complexity, 60-
61; and value, 27-28; Varieties of
Religious Experience, 27-28, 99
Jarrell, Randall, 106
Job, 2
"Jonathan Edwards and the
Language of God," 124 n.22
Jonathan Edwards Moral Thought and
Its British Context, 24

Kant, Immanuel: and aestheticism,
78; "pietistic" liberalism derived
from, 6-7
Kartiganer, Donald, "Process and
Product: A Study of Modern
Literary Form," 113
Kingdom and Community: An
Anthropological Approach to
Civilization, 5, 116
Knight, Douglas, ed., Tradition and
Theology in the Old Testament, 5,
116

Kuklick, Bruce, 11; *The Rise of American Philosophy*, XI

Laurin, Robert B., 4, 116

Lee, Vernon, 138 n.20

Lentricchia, Frank, 48; *After the New Criticism*, 46, 81; *Criticism and Social Change*, 81; *Criticism and Social Change* as a model for American empirical theology, 114-116; his criticism of de Man, 81; in defense of Derrida, 46-47

Liberalism: defined, 6; "empirical," 6-12, 120 n.11; German, 6-7; "pietistic," 6-12, 69, 120 n.11; romantic, 69

Liberation theology, 117

Lilla, Mark, 80-81

Literary theory, X

Locke, John, 8-9, 11; *An Essay Concerning Human Understanding*, 22-25, 71; and Jonathan Edwards, 22-26

Loomer, Bernard, 10, 20, 68; and aesthetics, 99; and concept of "size," 33-34, 115; and the doctrine of God, 59; on inter-connectedness, 42; on the moral ambiguity of God, 85; and the "problem of evil," 127 n.68; and process theology, X; as a radical empiricist, 30, 32-34; and the religious sense of history, 37; and scientific historicism, 55; and the tropism toward complexity, 60

Luther, Martin, 13

Macintosh, Douglas Clyde, XI, 9; and pragmatism, 84

Man's Vision of God, 34-35

Mariani, Paul, 110

Martin, James Alfred, XI, 10

Marty, Martin, XII

Materialism: dialectical, 14; Spencer's, 9

Mathematics, historicism and, 54

Mathews, Shailer, 9; biblical scholarship and, 107-108; and empirical aesthetics, 99; and optimism, 67-69; and pragmatism, 84-85; and process theology, X, 38; radical empiricism implicit in the work of, 30; and the socio-historical method, 117

May, Henry, *The Enlightenment in America*, 8

Mead, George Herbert, 73

Meditations, 21

Meeks, Wayne, *The First Urban Christians: The Social World of the Apostle Paul*, 5, 116

Meland, Bernard, 20, 68; aesthetics, 99; and the doctrine of God, 59; and empirical theology, 10; and historicism, 37-38; and the pervasiveness of evil, 85; and the "problem of evil," 127 n.68; and process theology, X; as a radical empiricist, 30-32; *The Reawakening of the Christian Faith*, 37; and scientific historicism, 55; *The Seeds of Redemption*, 37; on Whitehead, 128 n.73

Meyer, Donald H., 101-102

Miller, J. Hillis, 15, 47

Miller, Perrry, 23-26

Miller, Randolph Crump, X, 10

Milligan, Charles, XI, 10

Modernism, 14; and the predicament of dualism, 46

The Modernist Impulse in American Protestantism, 120 n.11

Modes of Thought, 49, 53, 97

Monism: and deconstructionism, 66; the empirical liberals and, 8; James and, 28; accepted by pragmatists, 83

Munger, Theodore, 121 n.11

Myers, Max, 50

A *Natural Theology for Our Time*, 35
Neo-orthodoxy, 69, 71
New Criticism, 14-15
New Testament, 116
Newton, Isaac, 13
Niebuhr, H. Richard, IX, 10
Niebuhr, Reinhold: An *Interpretation of Christian Ethics*, 68; on liberal optimism, 68
Noth, Martin, A *History of the Pentateuchal Traditions*, 5

Ogden, Schubert, 35-36
Old Testament Theology, 116
Olson, Charles, 112-113
The Origin of the Species, 75

Paine, Thomas, 8
Paterson, 108-112
Phaedrus, 56
Philosophy and the Mirror of Nature, 15
Pierce, Charles Sanders, 57
"Pietistic" liberals, *see* liberalism, "pietistic"
Plato: and mathematics, 54; *Phaedrus*, 56
Positivism: and empiricism, 14; rejected by American religious empiricism, 20; Spencer's, 9
Post-modernism, IX; American religious empiricism and, 12-17; characterization of, 12; and interpretation, 14-17; and modernism, 12-14; and New Criticism, 14; in poetry, 15, 17
Potthoff, Harvey, 10
Pragmatism: and the Chicago School, 84-85; dualism, monism and, 82-83; James's, 17; and Douglas Clyde Macintosh, 84; "strong," 74-77; and the tragic sense, 69-85; valuational, 77-85; "weak," 72-74
Prigogine, Ilya, 59

"Process and Product: A Study of Modern Literary Form," 113
Process and Reality, 34, 49, 55, 90-91
Process philosophers, 83-85
Process theologians, 20, 83-85
Process theology, IX-XII; American empirical theology as, 113-114; and cosmology, 49; historicism not applied in, 36-39; and the influence of Sherburne, 136-137 n.6; not accorded attention by academic theologians, 34; rationalistic, 34-36; and Whitehead, 113
Prophesy Deliverance! An Afro-American Revolutionary Christianity, 80
Putnam, Hilary, 80; *Reason, Truth and History*, 16

Radical empiricism, X-XI, 19, 21-23; and dualism, 83-84; and the "problem of evil," 127 n.68; and W.C. Williams, 104
Raschke, Carl, 48
Rationalism: a priori, X; and historicism, 42; and interpretation, 13
Rauschenbush, Walter, 7
Realism, Niebuhr's, 68
Reason, Truth and History, 16
The Reawakening of the Christian Faith, 37
Relativity, 51
Religion in the Making, 49
A *Religious History of the American People*, 67
The Rise of American Philosophy, XI
Ritschl, Albrecht, 7
Romantic liberals, *see* Liberalism, romantic
Romanticism, 13
Rorty, Richard, X; *Consequences of Pragmatism*, 15-16, 78; *Philosophy and the Mirror of Nature*, 15; on

value, 78-80
Rousseau, Henri, 8
Royce, Josiah, 7, 11

Sandmel, Samuel, 4
Santayana, George, 84, 101
Scharlemann, Robert, 50
Schleiermacher, Friedrich, 6
Schelling, Friedrich, 7
Science and the Modern World, 105
Scroggs, Robin, 116
The Seeds of Redemption, 37
Segerstedt, Torny, 52
Sensationalism, 25
Shea, William, on John Dewey, 138
    n.30
Sherburne, Donald W., and dualism,
    137 n.9; influence of, 136-137
    n.6; A Whiteheadian Aesthetic:
    Some Implications of Whitehead's
    Metaphysical Speculation, 89-92
Shirley Jackson Case and the Chicago
    School, 107
Smith, Gerald Birney, 9, 68, 84
Smith, John E., 11
Smyth, Newman, 9
Society of Biblical Literature, 107
Spencer, Herbert, 9
Stout, Jeffrey, The Flight from
    Authority: Religion, Morality and
    the Quest for Autonomy, 82
Subjectivism, 78-83
Suchocki, Marjorie, 114
Symbolism, 14-15
Symbolism: Its Meaning and Effect, 49,
    97

Taylor, Mark C., 48, 50;
    Deconstruction Theology, 48;
    Erring: A Postmodern A/theology,
    48
Theology, see American empirical
    theology
Theology in America, IX
Tillich, Paul, 7, 56; Dynamics of

Faith, 121, n.13
Tomas, Vincent, "The Modernity of
    Jonathan Edwards," 124, n.22
Towards a New American Poetics, 15
Tracy, David, XII
Tradition and Theology in the Old
    Testament, 5, 116
"tradition history" approach, 3-5,
    116
Transcendentalism, American, 7, 69
The Tribes of Israel: A Sociology of the
    Religion of Liberated Israel, 5, 116
Troeltsch, Ernst, 7
Tropism, toward complexity, 60-63

Union Theological Seminary, XI, 10
Unitarianism, 9

Value: empirical appreciation of, 32;
    and pragmatism, 77-85
Van Duesen, Henry P., 120 n.11
Varieties of Religious Experience, 27-
    29, 99
Voltaire, 8
von Rad, Gerhard, 3-5; and the
    interpreting historian, 116; Old
    Testament Theology, 116

Wainwright, William J., "Jonathan
    Edwards and the Language of
    God," 124 n.22
The Waste Land, 102-103
Ways of Worldmaking, 16
West, Cornel, 107; and historicism,
    79-80; and post-modernism, 16;
    Prophesy Deliverance! An Afro-
    American Revolutionary
    Christianity, 80; on Rorty, 79-80
Wheeler, John, X, 16, 42; and
    deconstructionism, 51-55; and
    historicism, 51-55; on the
    orientation of historical change,
    59; and the participatory
    universe, 52-54; on relativism
    and absolutism, 131 n.34; and
    Whitehead, 53-54

White, Morton, 22

Whitehead, Alfred North, 20, 41; *Adventures of Ideas*, 97; and aesthetics, 87-99; and American religious empiricism, IX; contrasted with Hume, 105; his empiricist aesthetic, 92-98; *The Function of Reason*, 49; and historicism, 48-50; and individuality, 87; and the interpreting historian, 115; and John Wheeler, 53-54; and mathematics, 54; *Modes of Thought*, 49, 53, 97; and objective value, 82-83; and perception, 93-94; and process, 128 n.73; *Process and Reality*, 34, 49, 55, 90-91; and process theology, 113; as a radical empiricist, 28-29; and the radical empiricist aesthetic in religion, 98-99; his rationalistic aesthetic, 89-92; *Religion in the Making*, 49; *Science and the Modern World*, 105; *Symbolism: Its Meaning and Effect*, 49, 97; and the tropism toward complexity, 60; and W.C. Williams, 105-106

A Whiteheadian Aesthetic, 89

Wieman, Henry Nelson, X, 10, 20, 37, 59; as a radical empiricist, 30-31; and scientific historicism, 55

Williams, Daniel Day, XI, 1, 10

Williams, William Carlos, 81; and American religious empiricism, 105; and dualism, 105-106; his empirical aesthetic, 95-96; formal poetic techniques of, 102-106, 108-112, 117; idealism denied by, 103-104; *Paterson*, 108-112; and post-modernism, IX-X; as a radical empiricist, 104; "The Red Wheelbarrow," 95-96; and Whitehead, 105-106

Winquist, Charles, 48, 50

Yale critics, 15, 47-48

Yale School of Theology, IX

Yale theologians, XI, 10; and pragmatism, 84